MARGUERITE PATTEN

MICROWAVE FOR ONE

HAMLYN

Produced by New Leaf Productions, Ashford, Kent.

Photography by Mick Duff
Design by Jim Wire
Typeset by System Graphics Ltd., Folkestone
Series Editor: James M. Gibson

First published in 1987 by
Hamlyn Publishing
Michelin House, 81 Fulham Road,
London SW3 6RB

ISBN 0 600 326 993

Reprinted 1988

Printed by Mandarin Offset in Hong Kong

We would like to thank: NASONS of Canterbury for the loan of china, tablecloths, napkins and cutlery; Lakeland Plastics, Windermere, Cumbria, for supplying microwave dishes and accessories for photography; and Tricia Payne for her assistance during photography.

The food was prepared for photography by Nichola Palmer.

Ⓕ This symbol after the recipe title denotes the fact that the cooked dish can be frozen.

CONTENTS

COOKING FOR ONE

Cooking for one person can seem an unrewarding task. All too often people in this position are inclined to say, 'It is not worthwhile using several saucepans and heating a large conventional oven to cook such a small amount of food.' In consequence their health can suffer because they buy somewhat inadequate, and often expensive, ready-prepared foods.

If you live alone, or have a family in which members come home at various times and require single portion meals, you will find a microwave cooker an invaluable way of solving this problem. You can cook interesting and nutritious dishes from fresh ingredients – ranging from light snacks to complete meals. These often take only minutes to cook, saving time and fuel.

Frequently you can cook and serve the food in the same container, thus eliminating much time-consuming washing up. A microwave cooker also provides a speedy and simple way of defrosting and then reheating or cooking frozen foods.

CHOOSING A MICROWAVE COOKER

There are many microwave cookers from which to choose, so it should not be too difficult to find one that fulfills your particular needs. The following information is only a brief resumé of the kinds of microwaves available; detailed information is easily obtainable from electrical suppliers.

Fitted units
If you are replanning your kitchen, you could consider a fitted unit in which a microwave cooker is placed above a conventional oven; each cooker works quite independently. This unit would be a great asset if you are limited in the flat working space available.

Combination models
These look exactly like an ordinary microwave cooker, but the casing contains a combination of microwave oven and a small traditional conventional electric oven (often fan-assisted). Sometimes a grill is incorporated into the cooker too, so you have the facilities of three-way cooking. Although relatively expensive, this type of cooker would be a distinct asset if you do not want to use, or purchase, a conventional cooker. You would need some form of hotplate to supplement the combined cooker.

Portable microwave cookers
The cheaper model microwaves have limited power levels and no turntable. While you can cook most foods on a single power level, as the recipes in this book will show, there are times when it is a distinct advantage to choose lower or higher settings for greater versatility in cooking. If the model does not have a turntable, it does mean you need to turn the dishes from time to time during the cooking to ensure even heating. Naturally these simple microwave cookers are the most inexpensive.

A timer is incorporated into all microwave cookers. This is set when food is placed in the oven; it means the cooker is switched off at the end of the pre-determined cooking period. Some more costly cookers have an automatic timer. This enables you to preset the cooker to switch on whether you are at home or not.

Microwave cooker outputs
As you examine the various cookers, you will learn about the varying outputs of the models. This has a bearing on the cooking times. The timings given in the various recipes in this book are based upon a maximum power of 650 watts (known as FULL POWER in this book although some instruction books call it HIGH).

If you are using a cooker with a lower output, then you must increase the cooking time. An approximate guide is to add five seconds cooking time for every fifty watts below 650. If the recipe in this book states 'cook for 5 minutes,' for example, you would allow five minutes PLUS five seconds for a cooker with a 600 watt output, five minutes PLUS fifteen seconds for a cooker with a 500 watt output, or with a 700 watt output SUBTRACT five seconds*. When using the defrost setting (in which the output is generally reduced to about thirty per cent of the maximum output) you will need to make adjustments too. However, a number of the most up-to-date cookers have a device, often called an 'auto-sensor' that deals with defrosting. When using this type of cooker, you simply programme the weight of food to be defrosted and ignore the timer. The cooker works out the correct defrosting time.

The term ROAST given in the recipes for puddings and cakes on pages 52 and 53 means you choose the setting on your microwave cooker that gives approximately two-thirds of the full power.

The term SIMMER given in the recipes for a casserole on page 41 means you choose the setting that gives approximately half of the full power.

Microwave cookers can be put onto an ordinary working surface and used on a 13 amp socket. If you want the cooker to be truly portable, it is possible to purchase a special trolley for most cookers.

If you are used to cooking for a number of people and now find yourself dealing with just one-portion meals, you may find it initially slightly surprising that in a microwave a single portion of food takes appreciably less time than two, three or four portions.

*This time may not be quite sufficient. Some manufacturers say the time should be increased by ten per cent for each fifty watts. It is, however, better to undercook and then replace the food in the microwave cooker. All makes of cookers vary slightly in the speed of cooking, just as conventional cookers do.

CONTAINERS TO USE

You will find advice on the best dishes to use in the introduction to each section or in the particular recipe.

Although there are excellent containers on the market which are made especially for use in a microwave cooker, do not rush to buy a large selection of these before checking on the dishes and bowls you already possess.

Special microwave ware has the advantage that it can be used in the feezer as well as in the microwave cooker.

Do not use: *Metal containers* of any kind. The microwaves cannot penetrate through metal, so the food will not cook and the use of metal could damage the cooker. Check that there is no metal trim on any plates or dishes you plan to use, and discard metal tags often used to seal plastic bags.
Ordinary plastic containers could melt, but there are plenty of suitable plastic dishes made for microwave cookers.
Waxed paper could also melt.
Very fine china or glass could crack when food becomes very hot.
Aluminium Foil: If containers are covered with foil, the microwaves would fail to reach the food and this would not be adequately cooked; also the foil could harm the microwave cooker. You will find that the use of a small piece of foil is advised in certain cases in this book, i.e. when cooking fish (see page 24). Before using, check the manufacturer's instructions to see if that is permitted in your particular cooker.

You can use: *Ovenproof glassware* or flameproof ware, china, earthenware or pottery dishes and plates – providing there is no metal decoration or trim on these. Check also that cups or soup bowls do not have glued-on handles because the glue could melt.
Boil-in-the-bag pouches and roaster bags may be used if they are sealed with an elastic band or string.
Greaseproof paper or kitchen roll or pure cling film may also be used. Be sure to buy the kind of pure cling film suitable for cooking. Other cling films, suitable only for covering, can produce toxins or deposit undesirable plastics on food when heated.

You can put food on paper plates or in wooden containers into the cooker for a short cooking period, but these are not recommended for long-term use.

Sizes and shapes of containers

When you select a container choose one in which the food fits fairly snugly. If you have a dish or plate that is over-large, moist mixtures, such as a purée or sauce or

gravy, spread out during heating. This means that the outside edges of the mixture tend to become overcooked.

If you have a container too full, you will find that liquids boil over in a microwave cooker, just as they do in an ordinary saucepan. Fill the container only half full of a liquid mixture, such as sauce or porridge. A deep ovenproof jug is ideal for making a sauce or custard; the diameter is sufficiently large to allow you to stir the sauce during the cooking.

FIRST MICROWAVE COOKING

You will now be the owner of a microwave cooker, and you are ready to use it. No doubt you have been given helpful information by the staff in the shop where it was purchased and by your friends, and you will have read about the kind of foods you can cook.

All this is excellent preparation, but not quite the same as being left to deal with the cooker. It really is a great advantage to be cooking for one person only, for microwave cookers are particularly efficient in dealing with smaller portions although, of course, they are used for family meals too.

How will you start using the cooker? Why not make yourself a quick snack and a hot drink? These two simple operations will familiarize you with the way to open and close the cooker and use the timer. You then can proceed with cooking a fairly straightforward meal.

Why not use it when you are planning breakfast? The speed of cooking is a great advantage at that time of the day.

Ideas for easy drinks and snacks followed by breakfast dishes are on pages 8 to 19. Each chapter begins with simple ideas and working methods and then continues with more unusual ideas.

There are certain instructions that you need to follow, e.g. 'standing time'. In many instances you are advised to allow the food to stand for a short time after being in the microwave. This allows the cooking to continue.

Be sparing with seasoning, especially salt, when cooking in the microwave as seasonings tend to be more pronounced.

Less fat is required when cooking in a microwave cooker, so this is an ideal method of cooking for slimmers and the health conscious.

FREEZING AND DEFROSTING

In many cases it is important to defrost the food before cooking it in the microwave. The manufacturer's instruction manual for your particular cooker will give details regarding this, and you will find comments in some of the sections in this book about defrosting. The letter Ⓕ after the recipe title denotes the fact that the cooked dish can be frozen.

SNACKS AND SAVOURIES

When you make toasted sandwiches, Welsh Rarebit or other hot savouries on toast, you will need to combine the grill with microwave heating. Use the grill for making the toast, add the filling or topping, put the food on a suitable plate and heat in the microwave cooker on FULL POWER. Suggestions for interesting fillings and toppings appear on the following pages.

Egg dishes are ideal for a quick snack; in addition to the recipes on page 9 you will find basic egg dishes under Breakfast Dishes.

Single portions of frozen smoked haddock and kipper fillets are ideal for one person. Exact timings for microwave cooking are generally given on the packets, but an average time is mentioned under the recipes on page 15.

SNACKS ON TOAST

BEANS ON TOAST

Tip baked beans into a dish, cover and heat for 1 to 2 minutes. Put on toast or put the unheated beans on toast, coat with sliced or grated cheese and heat.

MUSHROOMS ON TOAST

If the mushrooms are small, they can be left whole; if large, slice fairly thickly. Heat 15 g/½ oz butter or margarine in a dish, add the mushrooms, turn in the fat. Cover the dish. 50 g/2 oz whole mushrooms take 1 to 1½ minutes; sliced take about 45 seconds to 1 minute. Allow to stand for 30 seconds, spoon on the toast. The flavour is excellent.

SARDINES ON TOAST

Put sardines on hot toast. Heat for ½ to 1 minute.

WELSH RAREBIT

Top toast with sliced cheese and heat for ½ to 1 minute or blend 50 to 75 g/2 to 3 oz grated Cheddar or other cooking cheese with 15 g/½ oz butter or margarine, a little ready-made mustard and a few drops Worcestershire sauce. Spread on toast and heat for ½ to 1 minute.

YORK RAREBIT

Put a slice of ham under the cheese mixture in the Welsh Rarebit recipe.

BACON AND CHEESE

Cook bacon (see page 14). When it is half cooked, add a thick slice of cheese and return to the microwave cooker until the cheese melts.

SPEEDY PIZZA

Butter a large slice of bread. Top with sliced tomatoes, chopped chives and a little dried oregano or marjoram and a thick layer of grated cheese. Put on a plate. Cook for 1 or 2 minutes on FULL POWER. Garnish with an olive and anchovy fillets or sardines.

Note: Leftover anchovy fillets or sardines can be used in Spaghetti alla Marinara (see page 12).

STUFFED FRANKFURTERS

Slit 2 Frankfurters, spread the split with a little mustard and fill with fingers of cheese. Wrap each Frankfurter in a streaky bacon rasher and secure with wooden cocktail sticks. Cook on FULL POWER for 1½ to 2 minutes.

STUFFED POTATO

Cook a jacket potato (see page 46). Halve and scoop out the pulp. Mash with a little butter or margarine, season lightly. Blend with grated cheese or diced cooked ham or bacon or flaked fish, and return to the potato case. Heat for 1 minute on FULL POWER.

Alternatively, cut a slice from the potato, scoop out the pulp, mash and season. Spoon back into the potato case to make a flan shape, fill this with an egg, pierce yolk, top with grated cheese, and bake for 2 minutes on FULL POWER.

You may also fill the centre with mixed vegetables or baked beans or canned or cooked minced meat. Heat for 1 to 2 minutes on FULL POWER.

STUFFED TOMATOES

Select 2 large tomatoes and cut a slice from the end opposite the stalk. Scoop out the pulp and chop finely. Fill the cases with one of these mixtures:

a) a few bread crumbs, grated cheese, chopped tomato pulp, chopped parsley, seasoning.

b) flaked cooked or canned fish or chopped prawns, chopped tomato pulp and seasoning.

c) 1 or 2 beaten eggs, seasoning, a few bread crumbs and chopped tomato pulp.

Cook for 2 minutes or until just softened on FULL POWER or 3 minutes on SIMMER (see page 47).

TOASTED SANDWICHES

1 to 1½ minutes at FULL POWER

These make an excellent light snack. The bread has to be toasted under the grill or in a toaster. Naturally, if you have a combination cooker that includes a grill, you can use this to toast the bread.

Prepare the filling before toasting the bread.

The essential of a good toasted sandwich is to have a deliciously moist filling. To make the filling moist, add sliced tomato or a little mayonnaise or soft curd or cream cheese to the basic ingredients.

The fillings are a splendid way of using up small portions of leftover food. These are some of the ingredients from which you can choose:–

Fish: mashed, canned or cooked fresh sardines, tuna, salmon, chopped prawns, flaked kipper or smoked salmon or cooked or smoked mackerel or trout. Drain away oil, if trying to slim, or use fish canned in brine. Add sliced cucumber as well as ingredients suggested above.

Meat: corned beef, sliced cooked sausages or Frankfurters, salami, chopped bacon and pickled red cabbage, chopped cooked ham and chutney or pitted prunes.

Vegetarian: baked beans (mash lightly), various kinds of cheese with pickle or chutney, cheese and chopped dates or nuts or chopped pineapple or sliced bananas.

Toast 2 or 4 slices of bread. Spread one side of each slice of toast with butter; low-spread fats are less suitable for heating. You can add a little yeast or beef extract if this blends well with the filling. Add the selected filling and top with the second slice of toast. Put on a plate. Top the sandwiches with a lattice of bacon strips or anchovy fillets or sliced tomatoes before heating. One sandwich takes approximately 1 minute; 2 sandwiches about 1½ minutes at FULL POWER. Garnish the hot sandwiches with crisp lettuce and watercress.

COOKING PASTA AND RICE

Although you do not save a lot of time when cooking pasta or rice in a microwave, the result is excellent. It is quicker to boil the water in a kettle, rather than heating it in the microwave cooker. The oil is not essential, but it keeps the strands of pasta and grains of rice separate and prevents the water boiling over.

PASTA Ⓕ

To each 50 g/2 oz pasta allow 900 ml/1½ pints boiling water plus ½ teaspoon salt and 1 teaspoon oil. Put the water, salt and oil into a casserole at least 2 litres/3½ pints in capacity and add the pasta. Turn spaghetti or other long pasta around in the boiling water until the strands curl and are covered with water. Cover the container and cook on FULL POWER. Turn the pasta with 2 spoons halfway through cooking. The average cooking time is about 2 minutes less than when using a saucepan, e.g.,

Macaroni (quick cooking type)	6 minutes
Noodles (small kind)	7 minutes
Spaghetti	9 minutes

Allow to stand after cooking for 2 minutes. Test, then strain and serve.

RICE Ⓕ

The modern way of cooking rice is in a relatively small amount of liquid. When following this method in a saucepan, you use varying amounts of water according to the type of rice; but in a microwave you need the same quantity of liquid for each 50 g/2 oz rice.

Put the rice with 275 ml/9 fl oz boiling water, ½ to 1 teaspoon oil and salt to taste into a bowl of at least 1.2 litres/2 pints capacity. Cover and cook on FULL POWER as follows:

Long grain	8 minutes
'Parboiled' long grain	9 minutes
Brown long grain	16 minutes*
Frozen cooked rice	2 minutes or as packet instructions

Allow to stand for 5 minutes, test and serve. If by chance a very small amount of liquid remains, strain the rice before serving. You will find the grains beautifully light and tender.

The liquid used for cooking rice can be varied. Try using stock for savoury dishes, or cook the rice in pineapple, orange or grapefruit juice. This blends well with a curry or, if sweetened, can be served as a dessert.

*Cooking time for brown rice may be 18 or 20 minutes. Check after 16 minutes and add more boiling water if necessary.

SPAGHETTI CARBONARA

Cook the spaghetti (see page 11) and strain well. Cut 2 rashers of bacon into small pieces, put into a small casserole, and heat on FULL POWER for 30 seconds. Add the spaghetti. Beat 1 or 2 eggs with 1 or 2 tablespoons milk. Add to the dish and stir well to blend. Cover and heat for 2 to 3 minutes on FULL POWER or until very hot. Top with grated cheese and chopped parsley.

SPAGHETTI ALLA MARINARA Ⓕ

Cook the spaghetti (see page 11) and strain well. Heat a small knob of butter in a small casserole on FULL POWER for 30 seconds, add the spaghetti plus any fish you have available (e.g. flaked cooked white fish, canned salmon or tuna, diced anchovy fillets, sardines or a few prawns). Cover and heat for 2 to 3 minutes on FULL POWER or until very hot. Top with grated cheese.

LASAGNA Ⓕ

Cook 50 to 75 g/2 to 3 oz lasagna or lasagna verdi (wide ribbon noodles) according to the instructions on page 11. Make the Bolognese Sauce (see page 43) and Cheese Sauce (see page 50). Arrange the pasta and sauces in layers in a shallow casserole, ending with the cheese sauce, plus a little grated cheese and crisp bread crumbs.

Cook for 5 minutes on FULL POWER. This gives 2 small portions for two people.

KEDGEREE

This mixture of rice and fish makes an excellent light meal. Cook 50 g/2 oz rice (see page 11) and smoked haddock (see page 15). Flake the fish. You can hard boil an egg by boiling. Heat a small knob of butter or margarine in a dish for 30 seconds on FULL POWER. Add the rice and fish, together with 1 to 2 tablespoons single cream or milk. Cover the dish. Heat for 3 minutes on FULL POWER, stir once or twice. Top with chopped parsley and chopped hard-boiled egg.

CHEESE AND VEGETABLE PILAFF Ⓕ

Cook 50 g/2 oz rice (see page 11). Heat 15 g/½ oz margarine or ½ tablespoon oil in a bowl on FULL POWER. Add 1 tablespoon water, the rice and 175 g/6 oz diced cooked vegetables. Cover and heat for 2 minutes, stir to blend, then add 50 g/2 oz diced or grated cheese, 1 tablespoon chopped parsley, 1 tablespoon pine or other nuts and 1 tablespoon sultanas. Cover again and heat for 1 or 2 minutes.

Variations

LIVER PILAFF Ⓕ

Heat 25 g/1 oz margarine or 1 tablespoon oil and add 100 g/4 oz diced raw lamb's or calves liver instead of the vegetables. Continue as above but omit the cheese.

HAM AND CORN PILAFF Ⓕ

Use 100 g/4 oz diced cooked ham instead of the vegetables and sweet corn instead of cheese.

BREAKFAST DISHES

No time to prepare breakfast is a very usual complaint. The speed of cooking porridge or heating milk for cereals or producing a satisfying and appetizing cooked meal in a microwave cooker, however, should change your point of view.

Nutritionists frequently stress that a good meal at the start of a day is important. The method of cooking bacon, described on this page makes certain you do not have excess fat.

PORRIDGE

Cooking time: 2 to 2½ minutes at FULL POWER

25 g/1 oz quick cooking Quaker Oats
pinch salt
200-300 ml/7-10 fl oz cold water, depending on how stiff you like porridge
demerara sugar (optional)

Put the ingredients except the sugar into a deep cereal bowl or small basin and blend together. Do not cover. Cook for 2 minutes at FULL POWER. Check and continue cooking if a softer porridge is required. Sprinkle with sugar if desired.

Note: Different makes of rolled oats vary in their cooking time. If using thicker rolled oats, you will need longer cooking and a little more water.

BACON

Cooking time: 1 to 2 minutes at FULL POWER

In order to avoid excess fat, cover the plate on which the bacon is to be cooked and served with absorbent kitchen paper. If this is thin, it can stick to the bacon, so crumple it slightly. Place 1 or 2 bacon rashers on the paper and cook on FULL POWER for 1 minute or until as crisp as you like.

You can cook the bacon on a plate without kitchen paper. Either lift onto a second plate, or drain off the excess fat before serving.

Variations

BACON AND 'FRIED' EGG

While you can produce a 'fried' egg in the microwave cooker, it is not as good as when cooked by conventional means. You should cook the bacon as above for 30 seconds using a plate, but no absorbent paper. Break the egg into the small amount of fat on the plate, prick the yolk in 2 places with the tip of a knife to prevent it from 'exploding' while cooking. Return the plate with both bacon and egg to the microwave on FULL POWER and cook for 45 seconds or until bacon and egg are ready.

BACON AND SCRAMBLED EGG

Cook the eggs (see page 18) for 1 minute or less. Remove from the cooker and leave standing in a covered container. Cook the bacon. Check that the eggs are sufficiently cooked; if not return to the cooker for a few seconds.

BACON AND MUSHROOMS

Cook the mushrooms (see page 8) but allow only 1 minute cooking time. Remove from the cooker and keep covered. Cook the bacon and reheat the mushrooms for a few seconds if necessary.

BACON AND TOMATOES

Halve the tomatoes and season lightly if desired. Place on the plate with the bacon and cook together. For more lightly cooked tomatoes, add halfway through the cooking period.

BACON AND SAUSAGES

One sausage takes approximately 2 minutes cooking, but in a conventional microwave looks very pale. It is therefore a good idea to cook the sausage in the microwave for 2 minutes, then put it under the grill while cooking the bacon. Do not overcook the sausages because they become leathery and inedible.

KIPPERS

Cooking time: 4 minutes at FULL POWER

If fresh kippers seem a little salty when cooked in the microwave cooker, soak in cold water first or pour boiling water over them, drain and dry. Place a whole kipper or 2 kipper fillets onto a shallow dish or large plate. Top with 15 g/½ oz butter or margarine. Cover with cling film and cook for 4 minutes at FULL POWER. Test after about 3½ minutes, as the thickness of the fish varies. Allow to stand for 1 or 2 minutes before serving. Serve with wholemeal bread and butter.

Variations

POACHED KIPPERS

Put the kipper or kipper fillets into the dish with enough boiling water to cover. Cover and cook as above. It is worthwhile cooking more than one kipper and using the remainder for Kipper Pâté (see page 29).

POACHED HADDOCK

Following the method above, cook 100 g/4 oz of smoked haddock using milk in place of water. Check carefully as the thickness of fish varies. The haddock can be topped with a poached egg. It is worthwhile cooking extra smoked haddock to make a Kedgeree (see page 13).

FROZEN KIPPERS AND SMOKED HADDOCK

Follow the instructions on the packets. These fish generally take about 6 minutes on FULL POWER.

COOKING EGGS

Never try to 'boil' an egg in its shell in the microwave cooker. It will explode. You can produce excellent scrambled eggs, good omelettes, baked and poached eggs. It is quite possible to produce a version of 'fried egg' too. As eggs cook so quickly, and as we all have definite ideas on how well cooked we like them, check the cooking time carefully.

OMELETTE

Cooking time: 2 to 2½ minutes at FULL POWER

15 g/½ oz butter
2 eggs
½ to 1 tablespoon water (optional)
salt and freshly ground black pepper

An ovenproof or special microwave flan dish about 18 cm/7 inches in diameter is ideal for making an omelette. Heat the butter for about 30 seconds. Beat the eggs with the water and seasoning (the water is not essential but makes a lighter omelette). Pour the eggs into the hot butter and heat in the microwave oven on FULL POWER for about 30 seconds or until the edges of the omelette begin to set. Tilt the dish and loosen the eggs from the sides; this allows the liquid egg to flow underneath. Return to the cooker until set to personal taste. Fold or roll and serve.

Variations

SAVOURY OMELETTE

Add grated cheese, chopped herbs or chopped cooked mushrooms to the eggs before cooking or fill the cooked omelette with cooked ham, chicken, fish or mixed vegetables before folding. If the omelette is very lightly set, you can add the filling, roll the omelette and place it back in the microwave cooker for about 30 seconds to heat the filling.

SPANISH OMELETTE

Heat 25 g/1 oz butter or 1 tablespoon oil in the dish, add mixed diced cooked vegetables and heat before adding the eggs; or cook finely chopped raw onion, a crushed garlic clove, a little diced red or green peppers and diced tomato in the butter or oil before adding the eggs. Then cook until firm. Do not fold.

SWEET OMELETTE

Use milk or cream instead of water, omit the seasoning and add 1 to 2 teaspoons sugar. Cook as with the basic recipe, fill with jam or fruit purée, fold and heat for 30 seconds. Top with a little sifted icing sugar and serve.

FRUITY OMELETTE

Cook diced apple or fresh diced pineapple or heat a sliced fresh or canned peach or chopped apricots in the butter. Add the sweetened eggs and cook as in the basic recipe.

BAKED EGGS

These cook well in the microwave cooker. Put 2 teaspoons milk or cream into an individual ramekin dish, or heat a little butter. Break in an egg, pierce the yolk in two places with the tip of a knife. Top with a little milk or cream, season lightly. Cook for about 2 minutes on FULL POWER for a lightly set egg, or longer for a hard-boiled egg. This is an adaptable recipe. You can add grated cheese or chopped asparagus tips or put flaked tuna or sardines or salmon or diced chicken or cooked spinach at the bottom of the dish then proceed as above. The baked egg can be topped with 2 anchovy fillets just before serving. Eat with a teaspoon.

POACHED EGG ON TOAST

Cooking time: 1 minute at FULL POWER after water boils

1 or 2 slices of bread
little butter or margarine
150 ml/¼ pint water
salt
few drops vinegar (optional)
1 egg

Choose a small soufflé dish in which to poach the egg. Either heat the water in a kettle and pour into the dish or heat the water in the microwave. Add the salt and vinegar. The water should be at boiling point. Break the egg into the dish and pierce the yolk in two places with the tip of a knife. Cover the dish. Cook the egg for 1 minute at FULL POWER, or to personal taste. While the egg is cooking, toast the bread by conventional means and spread with butter or margarine. It is advisable to remove the dish from the microwave and allow the egg to stand for a few seconds. Lift out of the dish with a perforated spoon and put onto the toast. If cooking two eggs, use two small dishes. Increase the cooking time to 1½ minutes.

EGGS FLORENTINE

Cook and chop spinach; put into a dish. Make 150 ml/¼ pint Cheese Sauce (see page 50). Poach the egg or eggs. Lift onto the spinach, coat with the sauce and heat in the microwave cooker for 1 to 2 minutes.

SCRAMBLED EGGS ON TOAST

Cooking time: 1½ to 2 minutes at FULL POWER

These do not stick to the cooking utensil and have an excellent texture and taste.

1 or 2 slices of bread
25 g/1 oz butter or margarine
2 eggs
1 to 2 tablespoons milk
salt and freshly ground black pepper

Toast the bread under a grill or in a toaster and spread with half the butter or margarine; do this while the eggs are cooking and keep hot. Put the remaining butter or margarine into a jug or small basin and heat for approximately 20 seconds in the microwave cooker on FULL POWER but do not overheat. Break the eggs into the fat, add the milk and a little seasoning. Beat with a fork. Cook for 30 to 45 seconds, remove from the cooker and stir with the fork. Return to the cooker until nearly set. Cover and allow to stand. Stir before serving.

Variations

CHEESY EGGS

Add 25 g/1 oz grated cheese to the eggs when half cooked.

HERBY SCRAMBLED EGGS

Add lots of freshly chopped parsley and chives to the eggs halfway through the cooking period.

PIPERADE

Skin and chop a tomato, peel and finely chop a tiny onion, dice a small piece of red or green pepper. Heat the butter or margarine as in the basic recipe, add the vegetables and turn in the fat. Cover and cook for 1 minute. Add the eggs but no milk. Blend with the vegetables; season lightly. Cook as above.

SCRAMBLED EGGS AND SMOKED FISH

Hot or cold scrambled eggs make an excellent accompaniment to smoked mackerel, trout or salmon.

SLIMMERS SCRAMBLED EGGS

Omit the butter or margarine. Beat the eggs with skimmed milk and cook as above.

VEGETABLE SCRAMBLE

Blend about 75 g/3 oz cooked vegetables with the hot fat. Cover and heat for 30 seconds; then add the eggs and milk. Continue as in the basic recipe.

HOT ROLLS

You can heat rolls or croissants for breakfast in your microwave. If yeast or other baked goods are overheated, they become hard and inedible, so check the timing carefully. It is best to use a DEFROST or SIMMER setting. Wrap the roll(s) in absorbent kitchen paper. Allow just about 15 to 20 seconds on DEFROST and 20 to 25 seconds on SIMMER for one roll. Allow 40 to 50 seconds for two rolls.

DRINKS

It is very simple to prepare a beverage, such as tea, coffee or chocolate, in a microwave cooker, and it saves heating excess liquid in a kettle or dirtying a saucepan. Select the cup or mug carefully. Check that it does not have a golden or silver rim or any metallic trimming. Put a teabag and cold water into the mug or blend the instant coffee or cocoa or chocolate powder with cold water or milk. Put into the microwave cooker. Use FULL POWER.

If using a breakfast cup, which holds approximately 300 ml/½ pint liquid, allow 2 minutes heating in a cooker with 650 watt output. This gives a comfortable heat for drinking.

If you prefer to use ground coffee, put 2 level tablespoons coffee into a deep jug or ceramic coffee pot. Add 300 ml/½ pint cold water. Heat for 2½ to 3 minutes. Allow to stand for 1 minute; strain into a cup. If using boiling water, heat for about 1 minute so that the coffee gains more strength.

If a drink has become cold with standing, simply put it back into the cooker for a few seconds to reheat.

You can use the microwave cooker for preparing hot party drinks such as punch and mulled ale and for making lemonade and orangeade.

SOUPS

Soups are satisfying and economical, plus a splendid way of using up 'oddments' of food. There are a range of simple soups that can be prepared for one person. Some suggestions, which you could adapt for other foods, are given on the following pages.

You will find soups which can be served hot or cold on page 22 and others which are ideal for a main meal on page 23.

Use your microwave cooker to reheat canned or dehydrated soups or to prepare stock from the bones of chicken or meat. This will save the expense of buying stock cubes.

To make stock
Put the bone or bones into a large ovenproof bowl; cover with boiling water (it is quicker to use a kettle for heating water); add a little seasoning and cover. Allow at least 15 to 20 minutes on FULL POWER, strain and cool. Store the stock in the refrigerator or freeze it in small containers – an ice tray is ideal. Simply take out one or two cubes as required.

Freezing soups
All soups marked Ⓕ freeze well, so you may like to prepare an extra quantity and freeze this in suitable containers. If you line each container with foil, you can remove the soup when frozen and wrap it securely. Simply unwrap the block of soup, put it back into the original dish then defrost and heat. Stir after 2 minutes to ensure even defrosting. Remember to remove all foil before putting into the microwave. You can, of course, freeze soup in small 'boil in the bag' containers then defrost and reheat the soup in the bag in the microwave cooker. Remember to use string and not a metal tag to seal the bag.

Easy flavourings
Do not over-season mixtures to be cooked by microwave. You will find containers of crushed garlic or garlic salt a good alternative to buying heads of garlic. These store well. Dehydrated onion may be more convenient than buying fresh onions. Reconstitute according to the packet instructions. You can also use spring onions in cooking instead of larger onions.

Heating ready-prepared soups
Canned Soup: Pour the required amount of soup into a deep soup cup, bowl or ovenproof jug (do not overfill the container). Stir gently to blend the ingredients, cover and heat for 3 to 4 minutes on FULL POWER. Stir and serve.

Condensed Canned Soup: Dilute the soup as instructed then proceed as on page 20.
Dehydrated Soup: Measure out sufficient soup mix powder, gradually blend in the recommended amount of liquid. Allow to stand for 10 to 15 minutes for the ingredients to swell (unless it is the type of soup mix known as 'instant'). Stir well, cover and heat as for canned soup but stir at least once during the heating period.
Home-made Soup: Heat as for canned soup.

ONION SOUP Ⓕ

Cooking time: 7 to 8 minutes at FULL POWER

15 g/½ oz butter
2 medium onions, finely chopped
1 garlic clove, crushed
225 ml/7½ fl oz beef stock
salt and freshly ground black pepper

Heat the butter in a soufflé dish or basin, add the onions and garlic, cover and cook for 3 to 4 minutes on FULL POWER until softened. Add the stock, stir to blend with the onion mixture. Heat for 4 minutes and season to taste. If the soup has insufficient flavour, add a little yeast extract or brown sherry.

Variations

FRENCH ONION SOUP

Add a round of French bread, top with grated Gruyère or Cheddar cheese. Return to the cooker for 30 seconds.

CLEAR MUSHROOM SOUP Ⓕ

Use 1 onion and 2 to 3 large finely chopped mushrooms; omit the garlic. Follow directions for Onion Soup. Flavour with a few drops of Worcestershire sauce.

CLEAR VEGETABLE SOUP Ⓕ

Use 1 small onion, plus 100 g/4 oz mixed vegetables, e.g., grated carrot, a few frozen peas and frozen sweet corn. Cook the onion as above. Add the stock and remaining vegetables. Cook for 4 to 5 minutes on FULL POWER.

ASPARAGUS CREAM Ⓕ

Finely chop 6 canned or tender cooked asparagus spears. Peel and grate 1 small potato and 1 small onion. Put the potato and onion into a bowl with 150 ml/¼ pint chicken stock or water and ¼ chicken stock cube; season lightly. Cover and cook for 3 minutes.

To serve hot: Add the asparagus and 3 tablespoons single or double cream, heat for 1 minute then serve.

To serve cold: Allow the potato and onion mixture to cool, add the asparagus; sieve or liquidize the soup. Blend in the cream, dilute with milk if a little thick.

For variety use 2 or 3 chopped cooked or canned artichoke hearts instead of asparagus.

CUCUMBER AND MINT SOUP Ⓕ

Peel and grate or chop 100 g/4 oz cucumber and 1 or 2 spring onions. Heat 15 g/½ oz butter in a small bowl, add the cucumber and onion(s), heat for 1 minute on FULL POWER. Add 150 ml/¼ pint chicken stock or water and ¼ of a chicken stock cube, a sprig of mint and a little seasoning. Cover and cook for 2 to 3 minutes.

To serve cold: Cool, then remove the mint and add 3 tablespoons single cream or yogurt and top with chopped mint.

To serve hot: Remove the mint, add the cream or yogurt and heat for ½ to 1 minute. Top with chopped mint.

For variety, substitute peeled courgettes or a portion of marrow for the cucumber. A peeled chopped garlic clove could be added to give a stronger flavour.

SPEEDY VICHYSSOISE Ⓕ

Finely chop 1 medium leek. Mash a good sized cooked potato; blend this with 150 ml/¼ pint chicken stock and 6 tablespoons single cream or milk (you could substitute dehydrated potato). Heat 15 g/½ oz butter or margarine in a small bowl, add the leek and cook for 2 minutes on FULL POWER.

To serve hot: Add the potato mixture, season to taste and heat for 3 to 4 minutes. Top with chopped parsley and/or chives.

To serve cold: Blend the potato mixture and leek, chill well, then garnish. The soup can be liquidized if desired.

CHEESE AND VEGETABLE CHOWDER Ⓕ

Cooking time: 7 minutes at FULL POWER

15 g/½ oz butter or margarine
1 bacon rasher, derinded and chopped (vegetarians may omit this)
1 small onion, finely diced or grated
1 or 2 carrots, finely diced or grated
1 potato, finely diced or grated
150 ml/¼ pint chicken stock or water with a little yeast extract
salt and freshly ground black pepper
made mustard to taste
mixed herbs to taste
1 teaspoon cornflour
150 ml/¼ pint milk
few cooked peas or green beans (optional)
50 g/2 oz cheese, diced or grated

Heat the butter or margarine and the bacon rind in a bowl for 30 seconds. Add the bacon, onion, carrots and potato and turn in the fat. Heat for 1 minute then remove the bacon rind. Add the stock or water and yeast extract, seasonings and herbs. Cover and cook for 3 minutes. Blend the cornflour and milk, stir into the hot mixture. Heat for 2 minutes, stirring once. Add the peas or beans and cheese and heat for 30 seconds only.

Variations

FISH CHOWDER

Add 100 g/4 oz skinned and diced uncooked cod or other fish with the onion and other vegetables in the basic recipe. Omit the cheese.

PRAWN CHOWDER

Add 50 g/2 oz peeled cooked prawns with the peas or green beans in the basic recipe. Omit the cheese.

SWEET CORN AND HAM CHOWDER

Omit the bacon in the basic recipe and increase the butter or margarine to 20 g/¾ oz. Add 2 or 3 tablespoons canned sweet corn and 25 to 50 g/1 to 2 oz diced lean ham with the peas or beans. Heat for 1 minute. The cheese can be omitted.

TOMATO BEAN CHOWDER

Substitute the chicken stock and milk with a 225-g/8-oz can of tomatoes or 2 or 4 skinned fresh tomatoes. Chop the tomatoes. Measure and add the liquid from the tomatoes plus enough water to make a total of 300 ml/½ pint. The cornflour and cheese can be omitted. Add 50 g/2 oz canned haricot or red kidney beans instead of the peas or green beans.

FISH

A microwave cooks fish very well; the flavour and texture is excellent, providing the recommended cooking time is not exceeded. Keep the dish containing the fish covered during cooking. If the fish is cooked for too long a period, it becomes tough, dry and hard.

One problem with cooking whole fish or fish fillets is to make certain the thinner parts are not cooked before the thicker portions. You can tuck the thinner tail end of a fillet under the centre to give even thickness or cover the thin portion of the fillet, or a whole fish, with a small piece of aluminium foil. This prevents the microwaves reaching that portion of the fish and stops it cooking. After one or two minutes remove the foil. You must check, though, that the use of foil is permitted in your particular cooker.

You may imagine the fish is inadequately cooked at the end of the period given in the recipes; you should, however, allow the fish to stand for one or two minutes after the microwave switches off as the cooking continues during this time. The fish will still remain hot. As the natural flavour of the fish is so well retained, you can use the minimum amount of butter or other fat in cooking.

Fish can be cooked in a small amount of butter or margarine as in Trout Meunière (see page 26) but you should never attempt shallow or deep frying of any food in the microwave cooker. If you buy a portion of fried fish and want to warm it through, simply place it on a large flat dish and heat for 1 minute. Do not overcook; otherwise you spoil the texture.

Cooking frozen fish

There is no need to defrost a single portion of fish; simply cook from the frozen state. If you have purchased a packet of plaice fillets, however, you may need to defrost for a very short time to separate the fillets. Large whole frozen fish are better defrosted before cooking. If you want to add a coating or allow various flavours to impregnate the flesh, it is best to defrost, drain and dry the fish before proceeding further.

Most manufacturers give the time of cooking frozen fish on the packet. Remember to reduce the time by about 50 per cent if cooking one instead of two portions.

Using leftover fish

Do not freeze cooked fish; it is spoiled if reheated. Use leftover cooked or canned fish in Spaghetti alla Marinara (see page 12), as a filling in an omelette (see page 16), in a

kedgeree (see page 13), in a pâté (see page 29), or in Seafood Scramble: Prepare scrambled eggs (see page 18). Add flaked cooked fish when the eggs begin to set.

BAKED FISH

This method of cooking fish is ideal in the microwave cooker. For a single portion of fish melt 15 g/½ oz or even a little less butter or margarine in a dish in the microwave. Brush the portion of fish with this. Add a little seasoning including a dusting of paprika to give colour to white fish.

Place in the 'buttery' dish; arrange a fillet of fish to give even thickness (see page 24). Cover the dish with a lid or with cling film (pierce this in one place with the tip of a knife). Cook on FULL POWER.

Single fresh (not frozen) thin fillets (75 g/3 oz) take 1½ to 2 minutes; thicker fillets, thin steaks or cutlets (100 g/4 oz), 2½ to 3 minutes; thick steaks or cutlets of fish (150 g/5 oz), 3 to 4 minutes; whole fish, up to 5 minutes. Allow to stand for 1 to 2 minutes before serving. To add interest to baked fish top the fish with sliced cucumber or tomato halfway through the cooking time.

Variations

ANCHOVY FISH

Omit salt from the baked fish recipe, but add a few drops of anchovy essence or sauce to the melted butter.

DEVILLED FISH

Blend a good pinch of curry powder plus 1 teaspoon Worcestershire sauce plus 2 or 3 drops of Tabasco sauce with the melted butter in the baked fish recipe.

SWEET AND SOUR FISH

About 30 seconds before the end of the cooking time remove the baked fish from the microwave. Blend ½ tablespoon sweet chutney with ½ tablespoon lemon juice or vinegar. Brush over the fish – do not cover – complete the cooking. Top the cooked fish with crisp crumbs and grated cheese and heat for 30 seconds.

TROUT MEUNIÈRE

Cooking time: 5 minutes at FULL POWER

20 g/¾ oz butter
1 fresh trout, defrosted if frozen and well dried
salt and freshly ground black pepper
2 teaspoons lemon juice or white wine vinegar
½ teaspoon capers
1 to 2 teaspoons chopped parsley

Heat the butter in a large shallow dish in the microwave. Add the trout and turn in the butter. Cover the dish. Cook for 3 minutes, turning over once during this period. Add the remainder of the ingredients, and cook for 1½ minutes or until the fish is almost tender. Allow to stand for 2 to 3 minutes.

You can cook the fish for 5 minutes, then remove it onto a hot plate, cover and allow to stand while heating the other ingredients for 30 seconds in any butter remaining in the dish. Spoon over the fish.

Variations

FISH MEUNIÈRE

A portion of any white fish can be cooked in the same way as the trout. Allow 2 minutes cooking time for thin fillets, 3 to 4 minutes for thicker cutlets. To give an interesting colour, blend a few drops of anchovy essence (in which case omit any salt) or tomato purée with the lemon juice or vinegar.

TROUT IN ALMONDS

Increase the butter to 25 g/1 oz. Heat, then add 2 teaspoons flaked blanched almonds. Cook for 30 seconds or until brown and remove the nuts. Add the lightly seasoned trout plus a squeeze of lemon juice. Cook for 4 minutes. Spoon the nuts over the fish and heat for 30 seconds.

POACHED FISH

This method of cooking can be used for white fish as well as for smoked fish. It is ideal for the latter, as cooking in liquid counteracts the salt flavour. Page 15 gives details of poaching kippers and smoked haddock.

White fish can be poached in water or milk or white wine or cider (you can dilute the wine with a little water). Allow about 4 tablespoons liquid to a portion of fish; more liquid is required for smoked fish (see page 15). Place the liquid into a dish and add the fish, plus any flavouring required. Cover with a lid or cling film pierced with the tip of a knife.

Allow the same cooking time as under Baked Fish (see page 25). If extra ingredients are added, such as mushrooms, increase the time by about 30 seconds. To add interest to poached fish, add 25 g/1 oz sliced or very small button mushrooms, a finely chopped tomato, or fresh or dried herbs, the most suitable being dill, fennel, crushed garlic or garlic salt, rosemary or tarragon.

The liquid used in poaching the fish can be used in a sauce (see page 62).

COOKING FISH ROE

All kinds of fish roe are excellent when cooked in the microwave. The good flavour, texture and shape of the roe are maintained.

Soft or hard herring roe can be cooked without defrosting, but should be gently moved on the dish once or twice during the cooking period to ensure that they are evenly cooked.

Allow approximately 175 g/6 oz roe for a main dish. Melt 15 g/½ oz butter or margarine in the dish to be used. Add the roe with a little seasoning. Soft roe are kept more moist if a tablespoon of milk is added. Make sure the roe are arranged in one layer only. Cover the dish and cook for 1 minute. Turn the roe; then cook for a further 1½ to 2 minutes (frozen roe need the longer period). Top with chopped parsley, and serve with lemon.

Hard herring roe can be defrosted, dried well, then coated with a little well seasoned flour and cooked as above omitting the milk. The roe are better if fairly dry.

Roe make a good dish served on buttered toast.

Variations

DEVILLED ROE

This is particularly suitable for hard herring roe. Melt the butter or margarine, blend in a good pinch of curry powder, 1 teaspoon Worcestershire sauce and a few drops soy sauce. Add the defrosted roe and cook as above.

GARLIC ROE

Use 25 g/1 oz butter. Heat this with a crushed or chopped garlic clove or a generous amount of garlic salt. Add the soft or hard roe and cook as above.

ROE MORNAY

Make Cheese Sauce (see page 50). Cook the roe for about 1½ minutes, blend with the sauce, and heat for 1 minute.

COD'S ROE

Fresh cod's roe is excellent when cooked with bacon rashers. The roe is obtainable ready-cooked from a fishmonger. Cut into slices. Lay 1 or 2 bacon rashers over the roe, and cook for 1 to 2 minutes on FULL POWER.

FISH PIE

Cook the fish as on page 25. Flake and mix with a little White or Cheese Sauce (see page 50). Use mayonnaise if you have no time to make a sauce. You can add a few diced cooked vegetables or peeled prawns to the moist fish mixture.

Return to the dish, top with mashed potato and crisp browned bread crumbs. Heat for 2 minutes on FULL POWER.

Grated cheese can be added to the topping about 30 seconds before serving.

COD AND MUSHROOM KEBABS

Buy approximately 175 to 225 g/6 to 8 oz thick cod cutlet; cut into 2.5-cm/1-inch dice. Put the diced fish on two wooden skewers with a small button mushroom between each piece of fish. Melt 15 g/½ oz butter or margarine in a small dish in the microwave cooker. Blend in 2 teaspoons lemon juice or soy sauce or tomato purée, depending on the flavour required, plus a little garlic salt and pepper. Brush over the fish and mushrooms. Put on a flat plate, cover and cook on FULL POWER for 2 minutes; then turn over the skewers and cook for another 1 minute. Allow to stand for 2 minutes.

PAPRIKA SALMON

Peel and thinly slice a small onion; skin and chop a large fresh tomato (or use 1 or 2 well drained canned tomatoes). Heat ½ tablespoon oil in a shallow dish, add the onion and tomato, cover and cook for 1 minute only. Put in a 150-g/5-oz cutlet of salmon; turn it in the onion mixture so that it becomes coated. Cover the dish and cook on FULL POWER for 3 minutes. Remove the fish from the dish. Blend ½ to 1 teaspoon paprika with 5 tablespoons single cream or yogurt. Blend with the onion mixture and add a little seasoning. Return the fish to the dish; turn over once. Cover and cook for 1 to 2 minutes. Allow to stand for 2 minutes.

Variations

PAPRIKA FISH

Use any white fish fillet(s) or cutlets in place of salmon in the above recipe. Adjust the cooking time according to the thickness of the fish.

PAPRIKA PRAWNS

Use large prawns instead of salmon in the Paprika Salmon recipe. These are generally sold ready cooked, so heat for 1 minute only instead of 3 minutes.

STUFFED PLAICE

Skin and chop 1 large tomato. Chop 2 or 3 mushrooms, and blend with the tomato. Add 2 teaspoons chopped parsley, 1 tablespoon soft bread crumbs, ½ teaspoon lemon juice, 1 teaspoon oil and a little seasoning. Spread on 2 small plaice fillets (these can be skinned if wished). Roll securely with the stuffing inside. Secure with wooden cocktail sticks. Put into a shallow dish, cover and cook at FULL POWER for 4 minutes. Allow to stand for 2 minutes.

Other fish fillets could be used instead of plaice or the stuffing could be pressed on top of cod or other white fish cutlets or put inside boned fresh trout.

SWEET AND SOUR FISH

Buy a 175-to-225-g/6-to-8-oz cutlet of cod or other white fish. Cut into small dice. Mix together 1 tablespoon red wine or brown malt vinegar, 1 tablespoon smooth sweet chutney, 4 tablespoons orange juice and 1 or 2 teaspoons soy sauce according to taste. Add the fish and leave for 2 hours; turn over once. Heat ½ tablespoon oil in a shallow dish, lift the fish from the marinade and turn in the oil. Cover and cook at FULL POWER for 1 minute. Blend ½ level teaspoon cornflour with the marinade, add to the hot fish, stir well. Cover and cook for 1 minute. Stir and cook for a further 1 minute or until the sauce has thickened. Allow to stand for 2 minutes.

A few tiny cocktail onions and 1 tablespoon diced cucumber or gherkin can be added just before the end of the cooking period.

KIPPER PÂTÉ

Cook a kipper (see page 15). Flake the flesh, discard all skin and bones; blend the fish with 25 g/1 oz melted butter or margarine, 1 crushed garlic clove, lemon juice and cayenne to taste. If the pâté is a little thick, add a small amount of yogurt or cream to soften. Serve with hot toast or as a sandwich filling.

MEAT AND POULTRY DISHES

Meat and poultry cook more quickly in a microwave than by conventional methods. The results are good, especially when cooking tender cuts of meat and young poultry. You will soon find you can adapt your own favourite recipes. When making a stew, for example, heat the meat and vegetables for a few minutes on FULL POWER; then add the liquid (you need only half as much as when cooking a stew in a saucepan) and reset to SIMMER. Most beef stews take about 1 hour at this setting.

Single portions

The first recipes deal with steak, chops and cutlets, for these are the most popular and sensible cuts when cooking for one person. There are a number of new ideas, so the food does not become monotonous. Brush these meats with melted fat or oil. This is better then putting small lumps of butter over it. You can reduce the amount of fat used when cooking in a microwave.

When cooking a steak or lean meat, place it on a plate and brush with the minimum of melted butter or oil. Cook for the time specified, turn and brush again on the second side. Chops that contain a fair amount of fat are better placed on a microwave (not a metal) rack or an upturned plate. Stand this in a roaster dish, so that the excess fat drips away. You can, of course, use a roaster bag for cooking the meat; this is particularly suitable for lean cuts. Pierce the bag to allow steam to escape and tie with string. Do not use a metal tag.

Liver is a meat that overcooks easily; you will find you get the best result if it is cooked on the DEFROST setting.

Chicken portions and the various cuts of turkey meat that are now available offer a great deal of variety for small families and those living alone. The meat is lean, so take care it does not become overcooked. The suggestions under the various meats can also be used with chicken.

A single chicken portion will take only about 3 minutes cooking on FULL POWER with a standing time of 3 minutes before serving. This time applies when the chicken is cooked without a lot of extra ingredients. Various flavourings, as suggested on pages 40 and 41, do not affect the cooking time. Turkey breast will take about the same time to cook.

Cooking a joint or poultry
It is far easier to cook a small joint in a microwave than in a conventional oven. The meat shrinks less and keeps a better shape, particularly if cooked in a roaster bag. The roaster bag should always be pierced with the tip of a knife to allow steam to escape and sealed with string when using it in a microwave. If you cover meat with cling film when roasting, this too should be pierced with a knife.

Different makes of microwave cookers have varying power controls. It is possible to roast meat on FULL POWER, and the times given right are based on this setting. You may, however, have a ROAST setting on your cooker. As this has less power, you will need to extend the cooking times a little.

A boned and rolled joint of even thickness will cook more evenly than irregular shaped joints; so a small piece of boned and rolled sirloin or rib or topside of beef or a boned best end of neck (rack) of lamb or a piece of pork or veal fillet would be a good joint for one person or when entertaining. You can also buy small turkey roasts that have a neat round shape.

In order that the microwaves circulate evenly around the joint, place it on a microwave rack or upturned plate and stand it in a roasting dish or fairly deep dish. This applies when the food is cooked in a roaster bag too. Halfway through the cooking time, turn the meat or the bag over to ensure even cooking.

When the cooking time has ended, remove the cling film or take the meat from the roaster bag. Place it on a sheet of foil, with the shiny side inwards, wrap securely and allow to stand for 10 to 12 minutes (if cooking a joint about 900 to 1350 g/2 to 3 lb). The meat continues to cook, and you will find it easier to carve. Open the foil and serve.

Approximate cooking times on FULL POWER are as follows:

Meat	Per 450 g/1 lb
Beef	5 to 6 minutes – rare
	6 to 7 minutes – medium
	7 to 8 minutes – well done
Chicken	7 to 8 minutes
Lamb	7 to 8 minutes – 'pink'
	9 to 10 minutes – well done
Pork	9 to 10 minutes
Turkey Roast	6 to 7 minutes
Veal	9 to 10 minutes

If the meat or poultry is stuffed, allow an extra minute per 450 g/1 lb.

Roasting a chicken or game bird

A small whole chicken makes two or more excellent meals for one person. Brush the bird with a little melted butter or a few drops of oil before putting into a roaster bag, or covering with cling film. To prevent wing tips becoming overcooked, cover these with a small piece of foil if this is permissable in your cooker. Cook the chicken for the timing given in the chart. Turn the bird halfway during the cooking period and remove the foil. Wrap and stand for 10 to 12 minutes before cutting.

A tender pigeon or small pheasant can also be roasted in the same way. Use the same cooking time as for chicken.

Quail are unexpectedly 'meaty'. Roast a single quail for about 5 minutes or two birds for 8 to 9 minutes. These tiny game birds are delicious if stuffed with pâté or with cottage or curd or cream cheese plus a few seeded grapes.

Browning

Browning is not as good as when the food is cooked in an oven, but you can put the cooked food under a grill for a minute or two. A roaster bag helps to colour the meat or poultry, but you may still find it a little pale for your taste. It is possible to buy microwave seasoning to give a pleasant brown colour, or you could use chopped herbs or paprika instead.

A special microwave dish is made that helps in browning. This is the only dish that can be preheated in the microwave without food. When the dish is hot, the food is placed in it. The utensil is fairly large and relatively expensive, however, so you may not feel that the cost is justified for one person. The recipes in this section, therefore, are designed to give a good colour and appetizing appearance to meats of all kinds without specialist equipment.

Defrosting and freezing

It is advisable to defrost meat and poultry before cooking; this is essential when cooking whole chickens or other birds.

If you want to freeze a number of chops, steaks or chicken portions, place these on a flat tray, freeze, then wrap. Separate the portions with a square of waxed or greaseproof or kitchen paper so that the portions do not stick together.

COOKING LIVER

Cooking time: from 1 minute at DEFROST

little butter
lamb's or calves liver

It is all too easy to overcook liver; and when it is overcooked, it becomes tough and hard. If you like liver 'pink' inside, use a short cooking time on the DEFROST setting.

Melt a little butter on a plate at FULL POWER or DEFROST. Add the liver and turn in the melted butter. Cover the plate. A large fairly thin slice of liver takes 1 minute on DEFROST; 2 slices about 1½ minutes. Well-cooked liver takes 2 minutes. Serve as soon as possible after cooking.

If you are having vegetables with the liver and plan to cook these in the microwave, they should be lightly cooked (see pages 44 to 47), removed from the cooker and left standing while you cook the liver.

Variations

LIVER AND BACON

Cook bacon on FULL POWER for 30 seconds to 1 minute (depending how well done you like it (see page 14). Top liver with a little butter. Place beside the bacon, cover, reset to DEFROST. Cook as above.

LIVER LYONNAISE

Peel 1 or 2 onions, cut into rings. Heat 15 g/½ oz butter in a deep plate or shallow dish, add the onions. Cover, and cook for 1½ to 2 minutes on FULL POWER. Add the liver, turn in the onions and fat. Cook as above on DEFROST.

STEAK

Brush a 150 g/5 oz fillet, rump or entrecôte steak with a little melted butter or a few drops of oil. Do not add salt, as this tends to draw out the meat juices, but you can add a shake of pepper. Cook in the microwave on FULL POWER for 1 to 2 minutes, depending upon how well you like steak cooked and the thickness of the meat. Turn the steak and brush the second side with melted butter or a few drops of oil. Cook for 1 to 2 minutes. Cover the meat with a piece of foil and allow to stand for 1 minute before serving. If you like steak 'rare', then make sure you use the lesser cooking time.

To add colour to steak, brush the second side of the steak with a little mustard before the final cooking, or top it with a little microwave seasoning (this gives a brown colour), or shake over a little paprika. You can, of course, add a garnish of sliced tomatoes a few seconds before the end of the cooking time or top the cooked meat with chopped parsley.

BOEUF STROGANOFF

Cut a small fillet steak into narrow ribbons. Peel and chop a small onion and crush a garlic clove. Heat 25 g/1 oz butter in a shallow dish. Add the onion and garlic, cover the dish, and cook for 1½ to 2 minutes on FULL POWER. Add the ribbons of steak and cook for 1 to 2 minutes (depending on how well you like steak cooked) on FULL POWER. Turn the steak around in the dish halfway through this cooking time. Blend a 150 ml/5 fl oz carton of yogurt with ½ to 1 teaspoon tomato purée, a pinch of paprika, salt and pepper. Add to the meat mixture and stir well. Cover the dish and cook for 1 minute. You can add a good pinch of curry powder or a little French mustard for extra flavour.

STEAK DIANE

Choose a large, thin sirloin or rump steak. Peel and finely chop a small onion. Heat 25 g/1 oz butter in a shallow dish. Add the onion. Cover the dish and cook for 1½ to 2 minutes on FULL POWER or until the onion is tender. Add the steak, cook for ½ to 1 minute; turn and cook for the same time on the second side. Add a few drops of Worcestershire sauce and 1 tablespoon brandy or red wine or port. Heat for a few seconds only. Cover the dish, allow to stand for ½ minute, then serve.

PEPPERED STEAK

Cook the steak on one side, turn, and brush with a little melted butter or a few drops of oil. Crush ½ to 1 teaspoon black or green peppercorns. Press into the meat. If you have no peppercorns, use a generous amount of coarsely ground black pepper. Continue cooking the steak as usual.

To make a more elaborate dish, cook the steak; lift onto a heated plate, cover with foil. Pour 4 tablespoons whipping or double cream into the dish in which the steak has been cooked, stir well to absorb any meat juices. Heat for 30 seconds, add ½ tablespoon brandy or dry sherry. Blend with the cream. Spoon over the peppered steak.

ROQUEFORT STEAK

Cook the steak on one side. Turn, brush with melted butter or a few drops of oil and cook on the second side until almost ready. Top with a slice of Roquefort cheese or other cooking cheese and continue cooking.

HAMBURGERS

Blend 175 g/6 oz good quality minced steak or lean chuck steak with a little salt and a good shake of pepper. 1 or 2 teaspoons grated onion and a pinch of dried herbs or 1 teaspoon freshly chopped herbs can be added. Form into 2 round cakes, about 1.5 cm/½ inch in thickness.

Home-made or bought hamburgers should be placed on a sheet of absorbent kitchen paper on a flat plate then covered with another sheet of kitchen paper or greaseproof paper. Cook on FULL POWER for 1 minute, turn and cook on the second side for 1 minute. This gives a fairly well-done hamburger, but you must adjust the cooking time to personal taste. Frozen hamburgers need not be defrosted before cooking, but they need a little longer cooking time.

Serve with vegetables as a main dish or in the traditional way in hamburger rolls. Split the hamburger rolls, put a burger in the centre, and heat for ½ minute for 1 roll and 1 minute for 2 rolls.

Hamburgers can be topped with slices of cheese, canned pineapple rings, or onion rings just before the end of the cooking time, or you can top the cooked hamburgers with tomato ketchup or your favourite relish or chutney or with salad.

LAMB

Melt a little butter on a plate and add the lamb. Cook for 3 minutes on FULL POWER; turn and cook for a further 3 minutes on the second side. This timing is ideal for 1 large 150-to-175-g/5-to-6-oz chop or 2 smaller ones, if you like lamb fairly well done. Lamb cutlets require about 2½ minutes on either side, but naturally the exact timing depends upon the thickness of the meat and whether you like lamb 'pink' inside or better cooked.

To add colour to lamb, cook on one side and partially cook on the second side. Then top the meat with microwave seasoning or a little fresh tomato purée or tomato or mushroom ketchup. Replace the meat in the microwave.

CRANBERRY NUT LAMB

Allow 1 tablespoon chopped cashew or peanuts or walnuts, 1 tablespoon soft bread crumbs and 1½ tablespoons cranberry sauce to 1 large or 2 smaller lamb chops or cutlets. Spread over the meat just 1 minute before the end of the cooking period and return to the microwave to complete cooking for 1½ minutes.

CRISP TOPPED LAMB

Blend 3 tablespoons coarsely crushed potato crisps, 1 tablespoon chopped parsley, 1 tablespoon chopped spring onions. Press over 1 large or 2 smaller lamb chops or cutlets 1 minute before the end of the cooking time. Complete the cooking, but allow 1½ minutes on FULL POWER.

GLAZED LAMB

Spread the top side of a lamb chop or cutlet with redcurrant or mint jelly about 30 seconds before the end of the cooking time, return to the microwave cooker for another 30 seconds.

STUFFED LAMB

Cook a lamb chop or cutlet on one side; then turn and cook for 1½ minutes on the second side. Top with your favourite stuffing. Do not put back into a roaster bag if using this. Allow about 2½ to 3 minutes to make sure both stuffing and meat are cooked.

SWEET-SOUR LAMB

Mixed 1 tablespoon thick honey, 1 tablespoon vinegar, 1½ teaspoons soy sauce and 1 teaspoon smooth sweet chutney or sweet pickle or tomato ketchup. Cook a lamb chop or cutlet on one side, turn and cook for 2½ minutes on the second side. Remove from the microwave, and coat both sides of the meat with the mixture. Return to the microwave and allow barely 1 minute cooking. Sweet mixtures can scorch easily.

VEAL

Always brush a veal chop or slice (escallope) with a fairly generous amount of butter before cooking and on turning the meat. To keep the flesh moist, cover veal either with cling film or by placing it into a roaster bag. Allow 3 to 3½ minutes on either side for a 150-to-175-g/5-to-6-oz veal chop and 1½ to 2 minutes on either side for a 100-to-150-g/4-to-5-oz escallope on FULL POWER.

The veal can be flavoured before cooking with a little grated orange or lemon rind and juice or herbs, rosemary being a particularly good choice. Veal can also be marinated in red wine before cooking. Most of the suggestions for giving flavour to steak (see pages 34 and 35) and lamb (see page 36) can also be used with veal.

WEINER SCHNITZEL

Cook the veal escallope on one side; turn and cook for 1 to 1½ minutes on the second side. Remove from the microwave and cool sufficiently to handle. Brush both sides with a very little beaten egg yolk or melted butter and coat in fine, crisp bread crumbs. Place a sheet of absorbent kitchen paper on a flat plate and add the coated veal. Do not cover. Cook for 1 minute. Top with a lemon slice and/or a little chopped hard-boiled egg and parsley.

PORK

Cut away the rind and any excess fat from a 150-to-175-g/5-to-6-oz pork chop. Snip any fat remaining, to prevent it curling badly and to encourage even cooking. Place the meat on a rack or an upturned plate and stand in a roasting dish. Do not cover pork. It is better that this is not placed into a roaster bag, unless you have discarded nearly all the fat. Cook for 3½ to 4 minutes on FULL POWER. Discard any fat that has fallen into the dish, for this absorbs the microwaves and slows up the cooking. Fat also splashes and spoils the microwave oven. Turn the meat and cook for 3½ to 4 minutes on the second side.

Pork blends well with sweet ingredients, so you can brush the meat with a little relish or ketchup or add apple rings or apple sauce or cranberry sauce just before the end of the cooking time. Pork can also be sprinkled with mixed spice before cooking.

Variations

BARBECUED PORK

Peel and thinly slice a medium onion and thickly slice 1 or 2 unpeeled dessert apples. Heat 15 g/½ oz fat in a dish (this can be pork fat, butter, margarine or oil). Add the onion and cook for 1 minute. Add the apple slices, cover and continue cooking for a further 2 minutes. Cut away the rind and excess fat from a pork chop and place in the dish of onions and apple. Do not use a rack. Cook for 3½ minutes on FULL POWER, then turn over. Add 1 teaspoon soy sauce, ½ teaspoon French mustard and 2 tablespoons cider to the onion and apple mixture. Season lightly and mix well. Cover the dish and cook for a further 4 minutes. Let stand for 2 minutes.

GLAZED PORK

A pork chop can be glazed, as suggested for lamb (see page 36), but use apple jelly instead of redcurrant or mint.

PAPRIKA PORK

Cook the chop on one side for 3½ to 4 minutes. Turn and spread with a little tomato purée and a sprinkling of paprika. Continue cooking for another 3½ to 4 minutes. Garnish with strips of canned red pepper or fresh red pepper and heat for 30 seconds.

PORK IN ORANGE AND CASHEW SAUCE

Cook the chop for 3 minutes on either side. Remove the rack and pork from the microwave. Discard any fat that has dripped into the roasting dish. Heat 2 tablespoons orange marmalade with 3 tablespoons orange juice for 1 minute. Add a pinch of cayenne and 1 tablespoon cashew nuts. Put the nearly cooked pork chop in the mixture, turn over once or twice so that it absorbs the orange flavour. Cover the dish. Cook on MEDIUM POWER for 1½ minutes; turn the meat and cook for a further 1½ minutes. Allow to stand for 2 minutes.

BACON CUTS FOR MAIN MEALS

You can cook bacon chops (thin back rashers) or gammon very successfully in the microwave. When cooking a bacon chop, cover a plate with absorbent kitchen paper, put on the chop, cover with more kitchen paper. Gammon, however, is a lean cut of bacon, so place it on the plate and brush with a little melted butter. It can be covered with kitchen paper to stop excess splashing in the oven. Allow approximately 3 minutes on either side on FULL POWER for a 150-to-175-g/5-to-6-oz serving. Leave to stand for 2 minutes before serving.

Bacon chops or gammon is excellent served with various fruits, so add a canned or fresh pineapple ring or several thick apple rings or a few cooked prunes or apricots to the bacon 1 minute before the end of the cooking time. These add colour as well as flavour.

ROSEMARY CHICKEN

25 g/1 oz butter
1 teaspoon chopped rosemary or ¼ to ½ teaspoon dried rosemary
freshly ground black pepper
1 chicken leg or wing or boneless chicken breast

Cream the butter with the rosemary and pepper. Make several slits in the chicken and spread half of the mixture in these slits. Heat the remaining butter mixture for a few seconds in the microwave. Put the chicken in a shallow dish and brush with the flavoured butter. Cover the dish and cook for 3 minutes on FULL POWER; allow to stand for 3 minutes. Serve any butter from the dish as a sauce.

Variations

DEVILLED CHICKEN

Using the basic chicken recipe, substitute ½ teaspoon curry powder and ½ teaspoon Worcestershire sauce for the rosemary.

GARLIC CHICKEN

Using the basic chicken recipe, substitute 1 or 2 crushed garlic cloves or a good amount of garlic salt for the rosemary.

LEMON CHICKEN

Using the basic chicken recipe, substitute ½ teaspoon grated lemon rind and 1 or 2 teaspoons lemon juice for the rosemary. To make a more elaborate dish, cook a boneless chicken breast, remove from the dish and heat a few tablespoons cream plus 1 tablespoon white vermouth. Slice the chicken, turn in the hot sauce and serve.

CHICKEN MEXICAINE Ⓕ

Cooking time: 24 minutes at FULL POWER and SIMMER

1 large chicken joint
½ tablespoon oil
1 medium onion, finely chopped
1 garlic clove, crushed
2 tomatoes, skinned and chopped
pinch of chilli powder
1 teaspoon cornflour
½ teaspoon tomato purée
225 ml/7½ fl oz water
1 teaspoon vinegar
2 tablespoons diced green pepper
½ tablespoon sultanas
50 g/2 oz canned red kidney beans, well drained
salt and freshly ground black pepper

Cut the meat from the chicken and dice it. Heat the oil in a small casserole, add the onion and garlic and heat for 1 minute on FULL POWER. Stir in the chicken pieces, turn in the onion mixture, and add the tomatoes. Cover the dish and heat for 2 minutes on FULL POWER. Blend the chilli powder, cornflour, tomato purée, water and vinegar. Add to the dish and stir well. Cover. Reset to SIMMER and cook for 15 minutes. Then add the remaining ingredients, cover and cook for 5 minutes. Serve with cooked rice or potatoes and a green salad.

Variations

BEEF MEXICAINE Ⓕ

In the above recipe use 100 g/4 oz diced stewing beef instead of chicken. Cook on FULL POWER for 5 minutes, then for 1 hour on SIMMER.

GOLDEN CHICKEN CASSEROLE Ⓕ

In the Chicken Mexicaine recipe omit the chilli powder, tomato purée, vinegar and beans, but add about 100 g/4 oz finely diced or grated carrots halfway through the simmering period.

MUSHROOM CHICKEN CASSEROLE Ⓕ

Using the Chicken Mexicaine recipe, omit the chilli powder, vinegar and beans. Add 50 to 75 g/2 to 3 oz button mushrooms instead of the canned beans.

TURKEY MEXICAINE Ⓕ

In the Chicken Mexicaine recipe use diced turkey meat instead of chicken.

SAVOURY MINCE Ⓕ

Use this basic minced meat recipe to fill pancakes or omelettes, to top toast or split and toasted rolls or jacket potatoes, to fill cooked marrow or courgettes, or as a sauce with cooked pasta or rice.

To make four different dishes, divide the Savoury Mince into four before the final cooking. After cooking for 7 minutes, three portions may be frozen and adapted to make different dishes.

25 g/1 oz butter or margarine
2 teaspoons oil
2 medium onions, finely chopped
2 medium tomatoes, skinned and chopped
1 or 2 garlic cloves, crushed (optional)
1 tablespoon flour
150 ml/¼ pint beef stock or water with ¼ beef stock cube
450 g/1 lb minced beef
salt and freshly ground black pepper

Heat the butter or margarine and oil in a large bowl. Add the onions, tomatoes and garlic. Cover and cook for 5 minutes on FULL POWER. Stir in the flour, stock or water and stock cube, the beef and seasoning. Cover and cook for a further 7 minutes on MEDIUM POWER, if dividing into 4 portions, or if serving as above, cook for a further 10 minutes. For variety cook a little chopped bacon with the onions and tomatoes.

Variations

SHEPHERD'S PIE Ⓕ

Put one portion of Savoury Mince into a pie dish. Top with creamy mashed potato. Cover this with a little grated cheese and crisp bread crumbs. Cook for 4 to 5 minutes on FULL POWER. (See also Beef Cobbler on page 61).

CURRIED MINCE AND RICE Ⓕ

Blend 2 teaspoons curry powder or paste plus a generous pinch of ground ginger with one portion of Savoury Mince. Add ½ tablespoon sultanas, 2 teaspoons desiccated coconut and 1 tablespoon extra stock or water or wine. Arrange a layer of cooked rice in a dish, top with the curried beef. Cover and cook for 5 minutes on FULL POWER.

BOLOGNESE SAUCE Ⓕ

Put one portion of Savoury Mince into a bowl. Add a small grated carrot, 1 or 2 teaspoons tomato purée and 2 finely chopped small mushrooms (if available). Flavour with 1 teaspoon chopped fresh mixed herbs or ¼ teaspoon dried herbs and 1½ tablespoons red wine or dry sherry. Cover and cook for 4 to 5 minutes on FULL POWER, stirring once or twice. This sauce can be used as a topping on spaghetti (see page 12) or as a filling in an omelette or pancakes. It is sufficient for 2 portions, or in Lasagna (see page 12).

If you omit the red wine or sherry it is an excellent filling for vol-au-vent cases or to serve on hot buttered toast.

CHILLI CON CARNE Ⓕ

Blend one portion of Savoury Mince with 2 teaspoons tomato purée, about ¼ teaspoon chilli powder (add this gradually as it is very hot) or use a few drops of Tabasco sauce instead, about 100 g/4 oz well-drained canned red kidney beans and 1 skinned chopped tomato. Cover and cook for 5 minutes on FULL POWER. Serve with cooked rice.

VEGETABLE DISHES

It is a good idea to use frozen vegetables for the first attempts at vegetable cookery since they are young and tender and of uniform size. The microwave cooking time, therefore, can be guaranteed. As you become more familiar with your microwave, you will be able to work out the ideal timing for fresh vegetables.

Vegetables retain important minerals and vitamins when cooked in a microwave. You need less liquid when cooking vegetables, so more flavour is retained, and you should achieve a pleasantly crisp and firm texture if you have timed the cooking correctly.

Microwave cooking of vegetables is ideal for one person. You can combine several different vegetables and cook them in just one bag or dish. If the basic cooking time of one of the vegetables is a little longer than the others, frequently this can be adjusted by cutting the longer-cooking vegetables into smaller pieces. Always try and arrange the vegetables in a single layer in the bag or dish.

You need little water with the vegetables. If they are being placed in a bag, you need add only 1 tablespoon water to 100 g/4 oz vegetables. If they are arranged in a dish, add 2 tablespoons liquid and cover the dish securely with cling film. Turn the bag over halfway through cooking or stir the vegetables if in a dish.

Salt or other seasonings should be added *after,* rather than *before,* cooking. The small amount of water means a definite reduction in the amount of salt needed.

The microwave cooking time for frozen vegetables is given on the packets. It is difficult to give exact cooking times for fresh vegetables since size and quality as well as quantity determine the cooking time. You need to check during cooking just as you would when cooking in a saucepan. As a guide, however, here are approximate times for cooking 100 g/4 oz of the following fresh vegetables based on cooking in a bag; allow a little longer if using a dish. Asparagus – 3 minutes; beans (broad) – 2 minutes; beans (runner, sliced) – 3 minutes; broccoli – 3 minutes; Brussels sprouts – 3 minutes; carrots (sliced) – 2 minutes; cauliflower (small florets) – 2 minutes; courgettes (sliced) – 2 minutes; leeks (sliced) – 1½ minutes; onions (thinly sliced) – 2 minutes; onion (1 medium whole) – 8 minutes; potatoes (cut into 40-g/1½-oz dice) – 3 to 4 minutes; potatoes (whole, baked) – 3½ to 4 minutes; spinach – 2 to 3 minutes; swedes or turnips or parsnips (cut into 25-g/1-oz pieces) – 6 minutes.

Use FULL POWER in each case and allow the vegetables to stand for 1 or 2 minutes before checking. The above times are on the low side, but they will prevent overcooking. During the standing times the vegetables continue to soften.

CAULIFLOWER NIÇOISE

Cooking time: 5 minutes at FULL POWER

100 g/4 oz cauliflower, divided into florets
½ tablespoon oil
1 onion, cut into thin rings
1 or 2 garlic cloves, crushed
2 fresh tomatoes, skinned and chopped with 2 tablespoons water or 2 or 3 canned tomatoes and 2 tablespoons liquid from the can
salt and freshly ground black pepper
few olives
little chopped parsley

Cook the cauliflower (see page 44) for 2 minutes; strain. Heat the oil in a dish. Add the onion and garlic, cover the dish and cook for 1 minute. Put in the tomatoes and water or liquid and cook for another 1 minute. Put in the cauliflower, heat for 1 minute, add seasoning, olives and parsley.

If you like firm cauliflower, prepare the onion and tomato mixture as above, then add small cauliflower florets and cook for 1 or 2 minutes. Other vegetables, such as small firm Brussels sprouts or sliced aubergine or courgettes, could be cooked in the same way.

VEGETABLES MORNAY

Make the Cheese Sauce (see page 50). Cook a selection of fresh or frozen vegetables; strain and blend with the sauce. Spoon into a dish, top with grated cheese and heat at FULL POWER for 1 or 2 minutes, depending on the heat of the sauce and vegetables.

JACKET POTATO

A jacket potato can form an excellent basis for a meal. Scrub the potato, dry it and prick the skin. Place it on a piece of absorbent kitchen paper or on a flat plate. If cooking a potato weighing about 175 g/6 oz, cook for 2 minutes on FULL POWER. Turn over and cook for 2 minutes.

To crisp the outside skin, brush the cooked potato with a little melted butter or margarine and place under a preheated grill, set at low, for 2 or 3 minutes.

Variations

CHEESE POTATO

Cook and halve the potato. Scoop out the pulp, mash with a little butter or margarine, add a generous amount of grated cheese and season to taste. Return the mixture to the skins and heat for 1 minute in the microwave.

BARBECUED POTATO

Peel and chop a medium onion and 1 garlic clove. Heat ½ tablespoon oil in a dish, fry the onion and garlic for 2 minutes at FULL POWER; add 1 teaspoon Worcestershire sauce, a pinch of curry powder and 2 or 3 tablespoons baked beans in tomato sauce. Cook and halve the potato. Scoop out the pulp and mash with a little butter or margarine and seasoning. Form the mashed potato into flan shapes in the skins. Spoon the onion mixture into the potato halves and heat for 1 minute.

CREAMED POTATO

A potato baked in its jacket produces a lovely smooth potato pulp. To make creamed potatoes, simply cut a slice from the potato, scoop the pulp out into a bowl, and mash with a small knob of butter or margarine, a little milk and seasoning. If the potato has become cold, cover the bowl and heat for ½ to 1 minute.

POTATO SALAD

The cooked potato can be diced without removing the skin, or you can skin and dice the potato. Blend with a little mayonnaise, while the potato is warm, plus a few drops of vinegar and salad oil. Add 2 teaspoons chopped parsley, plus 1 teaspoon grated onion or chopped spring onions or chives. Chill well before serving.

MUSHROOMS

Mushrooms can be cooked in a small amount of butter or margarine rather than using water as when cooking most vegetables. The cooking time will vary according to quantity and size and also how well you like mushrooms cooked (see page 8). The times given there produce lightly cooked mushrooms.

GARLIC MUSHROOMS

Select very small firm mushrooms. To 100 g/4 oz allow about 25 g/1 oz butter or margarine. Blend the margarine with 1 or 2 crushed garlic cloves or a generous amount of garlic salt, 1 or 2 tablespoons finely chopped parsley or fresh red pepper and seasoning. Remove the stalks from the mushrooms. Use these instead of whole mushrooms for the soup on page 21. Fill the mushroom caps with the butter mixture, put into a dish and cover with pierced cling film. Cook for 1 minute only on FULL POWER. These make a delicious party hors d'oeuvre for two or a light supper dish for one.

TOMATOES

Tomatoes cook perfectly in the microwave; they can be halved or cooked whole or filled with a stuffing. While the tomatoes can be cooked on FULL POWER, they keep a better shape if cooked on SIMMER. The cooking time for 2 medium tomatoes is approximately 15 to 20 seconds on FULL POWER and 30 seconds on SIMMER, but check carefully as the ripeness of the tomatoes affects the timing. For Stuffed Tomatoes, see page 9.

STIR-FRIED VEGETABLES

Cooking time: 3 minutes at FULL POWER

15 g/½ oz butter or ½ tablespoon oil
100 g/4 oz mixed vegetables, weight when prepared, cut into matchstick shapes
½ teaspoon cornflour
½ teaspoon soy sauce
½ teaspoon vinegar
2 tablespoons water
½ tablespoon sherry
salt and freshly ground black pepper
pinch of sugar

Although this is not quite the same as when vegetables are cooked in a wok or frying pan, it produces an interesting dish. Choose a mixture of vegetables that give contrasting colour as well as varying texture.

Heat the butter or oil in a small dish. Add the vegetables, cover and cook for 1 minute on FULL POWER. Turn the vegetables around; then cook for a further minute. Blend the cornflour with the remaining ingredients and pour over the vegetables. Heat for 1 minute. Stir again.

COOKING PULSES

The cooking time for dried beans, peas and lentils is shortened appreciably if you use a microwave cooker rather than a saucepan on top of a conventional cooker.

It is necessary to soak dried haricot, butter or other beans and split peas or chickpeas overnight in water to cover. Lentils can be cooked without soaking, but the recipe on page 49 is based upon soaking the lentils for 1 hour. If they are not soaked, then increase the microwave cooking time by 2 minutes.

To cook 100 g/4 oz dried haricot, butter or other beans or split peas or chickpeas, cover with 600 ml/1 pint water or tomato juice or stock and leave for 12 hours. Add only a little seasoning when cooking. You can add a chopped onion and/or garlic or chopped herbs. Cover the container and cook on FULL POWER for 30 minutes, stirring once or twice. At the end of this time the beans or peas should be tender. Allow to stand for several minutes; then strain and serve as a vegetable or use in a main dish.

Cooked beans make a delicious salad. Marinate the beans in a well-seasoned oil and vinegar dressing while hot. Allow to cool; then blend with a generous amount of freshly chopped parsley and other herbs. Serve on a bed of crisp lettuce and watercress. Top with chopped spring onions and/or sliced tomatoes.

BEAN STUFFED PEPPER

Cooking time: 3 minutes at FULL POWER

1 red or green pepper
1 large tomato
4 tablespoons cooked or canned haricot beans
½ tablespoon chopped chives or parsley
salt and freshly ground black pepper
2 tablespoons soft bread crumbs
2 tablespoons grated cheese

Halve the pepper lengthwise; remove the core and seeds. Put the halves into a dish, cover with cling film and cook for 1½ minutes at FULL POWER. Skin and chop the tomato, mix with the beans, chives or parsley and a little seasoning. Spoon into the pepper halves. Top with the bread crumbs and cheese. Return to the dish with the cheese coating uppermost. Do not cover. Cook for a further 1½ minutes at FULL POWER.

Cooked lentils or split peas can be used for variety instead of the beans, or blend cooked rice with finely chopped or minced ham or chicken instead of beans.

BEAN PÂTÉ Ⓕ

Serves 2
Cooking time: 35 minutes at FULL POWER

50 g/2 oz haricot beans
300 ml/½ pint water
1 medium onion, finely chopped
1 garlic clove, crushed
1 teaspoon finely chopped mixed fresh herbs or ½ teaspoon dried mixed herbs
salt and freshly ground black pepper
½ teaspoon French mustard
15 g/½ oz butter

Soak the beans in the water for 12 hours. Add the onion, garlic, herbs and a little seasoning. Cover the container and cook for 30 minutes at FULL POWER, stirring once or twice. Drain away any surplus liquid. Add the mustard and butter. Cover and cook for 5 minutes; then sieve or mash the mixture. Add any extra seasoning or herbs required. Serve cold with hot toast. The pâté freezes well for 3 or 4 weeks.

For variety add 25 g/1 oz chopped nuts or freshly grated coconut to the mixture; add 1 or 2 tablespoons freshly chopped parsley to the mixture; or use split peas instead of beans.

LENTIL CURRY

Cooking time: 10 minutes at FULL POWER

50 g/2 oz split lentils
150 ml/¼ pint water
15 g/½ oz margarine or ½ tablespoon oil
1 medium onion, finely chopped
½ to 1 tablespoon curry powder
salt and freshly ground black pepper
squeeze of lemon juice
1 tablespoon sultanas
2 teaspoons desiccated coconut (optional)

Cover the lentils with the water and allow to soak for 1 hour. Put the margarine or oil into a bowl and heat for 30 seconds; add the onion and curry powder and heat again for 30 seconds. Pour in the lentils and water; add a little seasoning and the lemon juice. Stir well to blend. Cover and cook for 8 minutes at FULL POWER, stirring once or twice during this time and checking the liquid. Add the sultanas and coconut and any extra seasoning required, cover and heat for a further 1 minute. Serve with chutney and chopped nuts and/or a Raita, made by blending diced cucumber with yogurt and a little chopped mint.

SAUCES

You will find it a great asset to cook small quantities of sauce in the microwave. The mixture does not stick to the container, and therefore you have no wastage. You must, however, stir well to blend the flour or cornflour with the liquid, and it is advisable to stir during the cooking period.

It is a good idea to keep a small stock of flavourings to add interest to savoury dishes. A tube of tomato purée or containers of garlic and onion salt (which can save buying garlic or onions) will flavour a small amount of sauce. A small but carefully selected herb garden or small containers of dried herbs help make your cooking interesting.

Worcestershire sauce is a great stand-by; anchovy essence (or sauce) adds interest to fish dishes. Soy sauce gives dishes a Chinese touch.

WHITE SAUCE

Cooking time: 2 minutes at FULL POWER

15 g/½ oz butter or margarine
15 g/½ oz flour
150 ml/¼ pint milk
salt and freshly ground black pepper

Put the butter or margarine into a basin or jug and heat for about 20 seconds at FULL POWER. Add the flour then the milk; stir well to blend. Retun to the cooker, heat for a further 30 seconds, and stir well to complete the cooking. Add the seasoning and stir briskly.

For variety use ½ level tablespoon cornflour instead of the flour, or add a little chopped parsley or other herbs or anchovy essence or chopped hard-boiled egg (cooked in a saucepan) or a few chopped prawns or sliced cooked mushrooms.

Variations

CHEESE SAUCE

Blend 25 to 50 g/1 to 2 oz grated cheese into the hot White Sauce. This should melt without reheating in the microwave cooker.

BROWN SAUCE

Use the same method as White Sauce, but substitute stock plus a little gravy, browning, or water with ¼ of a beef or chicken stock cube for the milk.

GRAVY

Use fat from roasting the meat instead of the butter in the White Sauce recipe and slightly less flour or cornflour to give a thinner consistency.

SPEEDY TOMATO SAUCE

Use tomato juice plus 1 teaspoon concentrated tomato purée instead of milk in the White Sauce recipe. Add a pinch of garlic salt to the thickened sauce and a shake of cayenne.

EASY ESPAGNOLE SAUCE

Cooking time: 4 minutes at FULL POWER

15 g/½ oz butter or margarine
2 small mushrooms, finely chopped
1 medium tomato, concassed*
1 small onion, finely chopped or grated
4 tablespoons water or chicken stock
1 tablespoon sherry
salt and freshly ground black pepper

Heat the butter or margarine for 30 seconds; then add the next four ingredients. Cover and heat for 3 minutes at FULL POWER, add the sherry and seasoning and heat for 30 seconds. Sieve or blend in a liquidizer if wished. Serve with savoury dishes.

*skinned, seeded and chopped.

SWEET SAUCES

It is easier to cook sweet sauces in the microwave cooker than in a saucepan. The sweet ingredients will not stick to a basin as they often do to a small saucepan. Remember that chocolate can overheat in a microwave just as when melted over hot water.

CHOCOLATE SAUCE (1)

Cooking time: 1 minute at FULL POWER

2 tablespoons water
1 tablespoon sugar
½ level tablespoon golden syrup
1 tablespoon cocoa powder
15 g/½ oz butter

Put all the ingredients into a small container and stir well to blend the cocoa with the water. Heat for 1 minute at FULL POWER; then stir well. Serve over ice cream or a peeled and cored dessert pear.

For variety you can use slightly more cocoa if you like a strong plain chocolate taste. Use 2 tablespoons chocolate powder and reduce the amount of sugar slightly. You may omit the syrup, but it does give a good texture to the sauce.

CHOCOLATE SAUCE (2)

Put 1 tablespoon water into a container. Break 50 g/2 oz plain or milk chocolate into pieces, add to the water and heat for 45 seconds on FULL POWER.

CARAMEL SAUCE

Cooking time: 6 minutes at FULL POWER

A caramel sauce is an excellent stand-by. It can be served over ice cream, or an egg custard or fruit. The sugar and water mixture is boiled to a very high temperature, so make quite sure the utensil used in the microwave cooker will withstand this heat. As this stores well in a screw topped jar (to exclude air), it is worth making a fair quantity.

100 g/4 oz granulated or caster sugar
150 ml/¼ pint water (8 tablespoons)

Put the sugar and half the water (4 tablespoons) into the strong utensil, heat for 30 seconds on FULL POWER. Stir well, then continue heating on FULL POWER until golden brown. Check the cooking once or twice, stirring if cooking unevenly. Allow to stand for 1 minute, then stir in the remaining 4 tablespoons water* to make a pouring sauce.

For a thicker caramel, use only 2 tablespoons water after making the caramel.

*Use hot water, especially if cooking in an ovenproof glass bowl.

PUDDINGS AND BAKING

The recipes in this section are planned to give interesting and varied desserts for one person. In a few instances double the amount of ingredients is given as the dish is equally good hot or cold. You can prepare sufficient dessert for two meals or divide the mixture to make a pudding and cake or cakes. As some recipes contain a high percentage of sugar, choose the cooking container carefully; it must be sufficiently strong to withstand the high temperature reached by a sugar mixture.

Sponge and suet puddings

Do not overcook a sponge or suet mixture; this makes it hard and tough. Check after three quarters of the way through the recommended cooking time and test carefully. The mixture should appear set around the edges but still slightly soft on the top. If in doubt, test with a fine skewer. When the pudding is done, the skewer should come out clean. The cooking is completed when the mixture stands after microwave cooking.

A pudding mixture can be lightly covered, just as when cooking a pudding in a steamer, but allow plenty of space for the pudding or cake to rise. Microwave cooking produces a mixture that rises appreciably more than when it is cooked by conventional means.

The setting recommended in the following recipes is ROAST, but if your particular cooker does not have this setting, use FULL POWER and shorten the cooking times given in the recipes.

Adding jam or syrup or honey

In the recipe below a teaspoon of honey or golden syrup is placed in each basin. This is very satisfactory as the moisture from the peach prevents the honey or syrup from burning. It is, however, inadvisable to put jam or syrup under a plain sponge or suet mixture as it will burn in the microwave cooker. Heat the sweet ingredient separately for a few seconds and spoon over the cooked pudding.

PEACH UPSIDE-DOWN PUDDINGS Ⓕ

Cooking time: 5 minutes at ROAST

For the base

2 halved canned peaches
2 teaspoons honey or golden syrup

For the sponge

50 g/2 oz butter or margarine
50 g/2 oz caster sugar
1 egg
50 g/2 oz self-raising flour
½ tablespoon milk

Lightly grease two individual basins of about 300 ml/½ pint capacity or breakfast cups. Do not use too small containers, as light mixtures tend to rise more when

cooked by microwave. Drain the peaches well and place a peach and half the honey or golden syrup into each basin. Cream the butter or margarine with the sugar, add the egg then the flour and milk. Spoon over the peaches. Cook the two puddings for 5 minutes on ROAST or until lightly set. Allow to stand for 2 minutes as the sponges continue to cook during the standing time. Turn out. Enjoy one pudding hot and the second pudding cold.

Variations

LEMON AND APRICOT PUDDINGS Ⓕ

Use 4 canned apricots instead of peaches and lemon marmalade instead of honey or syrup in the above recipe. Add ½ teaspoon grated lemon rind to the sponge mixture and use lemon juice instead of milk.

PEAR AND CHOCOLATE PUDDINGS Ⓕ

Use 2 sliced canned or ripe pear halves instead of peaches in the above recipe. Top with the honey or syrup. Use only 40 g/1½ oz flour, plus 15 g/½ oz chocolate powder in the sponge.

SPONGE PUDDING AND CAKES

Make the basic sponge mixture for Peach Upside-Down Puddings.

For the pudding

Use half the mixture. Place this into a lightly greased breakfast cup or 300-ml/½-pint basin. Cook for 1¼ to 1½ minutes on ROAST setting or just 1 minute on FULL POWER. Allow to stand for 2 minutes.

Meanwhile heat a little jam or syrup or lemon curd diluted with an equal amount of water or lemon or orange juice. Serve this as a sauce over the pudding.

For the cakes

Divide the remaining mixture into 5 paper cases. To help these keep a better shape, you can stand them in a microwave bun tray or use a double layer of paper cases. Cook for 2 minutes on ROAST setting or 1½ minutes on FULL POWER. Allow to stand for 1 to 2 minutes. Sprinkle with icing sugar and decorate with chocolate flake. For variety flavour the sponge mixture as in the recipe above or add about 25 g/1 oz dried fruit.

SUET PUDDING

It is possible to cook a suet pudding in minutes. To make one small suet pudding, blend 25 g/1 oz shredded suet and 25 g/1 oz brown sugar with 50 g/2 oz self-raising flour. Bind with enough milk to make a sticky dough. Put into a lightly greased 300-ml/½-pint basin. Cover the basin with cling film.

This suet pudding can be cooked on FULL POWER for 2 minutes, but it is lighter in texture if cooked for 4 minutes on SIMMER. Allow to stand for 2 minutes before turning out. Serve with hot jam or marmalade or fruit purée or custard sauce.

Variation

ORANGE PUDDING

To vary the basic Suet Pudding recipe, add 1 or 2 teaspoons grated orange rind and 1 tablespoon orange marmalade to the flour. Bind with orange juice instead of milk.

MILK PUDDINGS

A microwave cooker can be used for making custards and milk puddings.

A rice pudding is never as creamy as when prepared by conventional means, but this is the method to use. To increase the creamy texture of the pudding, use undiluted evaporated milk instead of fresh milk.

Put 50 g/2 oz short-grain rice into a good-sized pie dish or casserole or basin. Add 300 ml/½ pint milk and sugar to taste. Heat on FULL POWER for 2 to 3 minutes, or until the milk and rice are very hot. Stir well then reduce power to SIMMER and cook for 25 to 35 minutes. Makes of rice vary in the cooking time required, so check occasionally.

Variation

RICE CONDÉ

Cook the rice pudding as above. Serve half the pudding hot with cooked fruit. Allow the rest of the pudding to become quite cold. Blend in a little whipped cream. Spoon into a dish and top with fresh or cooked fruit.

Heat 1½ tablespoons redcurrant jelly with ½ tablespoon water for a few seconds in the microwave cooker on FULL POWER. Cool slightly then spoon over the fruit.

MAKING CUSTARD

With Custard Powder

Blend 1 level tablespoon custard powder with 300 ml/½ pint cold milk in a basin or deep jug for a pouring custard sauce. (Use a little more powder for the trifles on page 61). Cook for 2 minutes on FULL POWER. Stir well after 1 minute to keep the custard smooth. Add sugar to taste.

With Eggs

Beat 2 eggs in a basin or deep jug, with ½ to 1 tablespoon sugar. Add 300 ml/½ pint hot, but not boiling, milk and a few drops of vanilla essence. Cook for 4 minutes on MEDIUM POWER, beating every minute. At the end of this time the custard should be starting to thicken. Beat briskly and allow to stand for a few minutes. The custard will continue to thicken; you can return it to the microwave if it is not quite as thick as you would like.

For a thicker custard, more like baked custard, use 4 egg yolks or 2 whole eggs plus 1 egg yolk to the 300 ml/½ pint milk. Top the cooked custard with grated nutmeg just before serving. This method of making an egg custard tends to be more successful than cooking in a pie dish.

Variations

CUSTARD ROYALE

Make the thick custard as above. Divide into two small containers. Allow to cool. Top with a layer of strawberry jam and lightly whipped cream.

APPLE FOULE BRÛLÉE

Divide the custard into two flameproof containers. Smooth flat. Bake a large apple (see page 56), skin it and sweeten it slightly. Spread over the custard. Top with brown sugar. Place under a preheated grill set on low and leave for 1 or 2 minutes until the topping is crisp. Other fruits can be used for variety.

QUEEN OF PUDDINGS

Serves 2

To make the sauce

Make the Egg Custard Sauce (see left), but use 225 ml/7½ fl oz milk to 2 egg yolks; save the egg whites for the meringue. Stir 2 tablespoons fine cake crumbs, sweet biscuit crumbs or bread crumbs into the hot sauce, together with a little grated orange or lemon rind. Spread 2 teaspoons jam into a pie dish, add the custard mixture, smooth flat and top with more jam.

To make the meringue

Whisk the 2 egg whites until stiff. Fold in 75 g/3 oz caster sugar or light brown sugar. Spoon over the custard mixture and place in the microwave cooker. Cook for 2 minutes on FULL POWER. This microwave meringue has a texture rather like a marshmallow. Serve hot or cold.

COOKING FRUIT

Use the microwave for cooking fresh or dried fruit, for the results are excellent.

When cooking fresh fruit, use very little liquid, i.e., 1 tablespoon to each 225 g/8 oz soft fruit or 2 tablespoons to each 225 g/8 oz firm fruit, such as plums or sliced apples. Place the prepared fruit into a casserole with the water and a little sugar. Cover. Cook for 1 to 1½ minutes on FULL POWER for soft fruits and 2 to 2½ minutes for firm fruit. Allow to stand for 2 to 3 minutes.

When cooking dried fruit, such as prunes, cover the fruit with boiling water and allow to stand for several hours before cooking. Cook for 6 minutes on FULL POWER for 100 g/4 oz dried fruit. Allow to stand for 15 minutes before serving. You can reheat the fruit for 1 minute.

BAKED APPLE

The flesh of a baked apple is delicious when cooked in a microwave, but the skin tends to be less tender than when baked in the oven.

Core the apple and split the skin round the centre. Place the apple on a plate. Do not cover. Cook for 2½ to 3 minutes, depending upon the size of the apple. Allow to stand for 1 to 2 minutes.

The centre of the apple can be filled with sultanas or mincemeat before baking.

Variations

APRICOT APPLE

Bake the apple using the method above until nearly soft; then fill the centre with apricot jam and finely chopped blanched almonds. Continue cooking.

COCONUT APPLE

Cook the apple, using the method left. Take off the skin. Spread the pulp with a little raspberry jam; sprinkle with desiccated coconut. Return to the microwave for a further 30 seconds on FULL POWER.

APRICOT MOUSSE Ⓕ

Serves 2
Cooking time: ½ to ¾ minute at FULL POWER

½ tablespoon lemon juice
1½ tablespoons water
1½ teaspoons gelatine
300 ml/½ pint thick sweetened apricot purée from cooked or canned fresh or dried apricots
5 tablespoons double or whipping cream
1 egg white
sugar to taste (optional)

Put the lemon juice and water into a basin sufficiently large to use for incorporating the rest of the ingredients. Sprinkle the gelatine on top; allow to stand for 2 to 3 minutes without stirring. Place in the microwave

cooker at FULL POWER for ½ to ¾ minute until the gelatine has melted. Gelatine melts easily and successfully in a microwave cooker.

Stir in the apricot purée (see advice on cooking fruit left). Allow to cool and stiffen slightly. Whip the cream in one basin until it stand in peaks. Whisk the egg white in a second basin until stiff. Fold the cream and the egg white into the apricot mixture. Taste and add more sugar if desired. Spoon into 2 dishes and leave until firm. This does not become sufficiently firm to turn out like a mould.

The mousse can be topped with whipped cream and nuts or whole fruit. For variety use other fruits instead of apricots, Apple pulp (from baked apple) is excellent in this recipe. Use orange juice instead of water.

SIMPLE BAKING

You will find that scones bake well in the microwave cooker. They do not brown, although the use of brown sugar in sweet scones and cheese in a savoury mixture helps to give a slight tint. If you have a browning dish, you can preheat this for about 8 minutes. Bake the scones for about 2 minutes, turn and cook for a further 1 minute to give the effect of griddle scones.

While there is no question that pastry is better baked in a conventional oven, you may find it useful to cook small amounts in the microwave. Always check the cooking process in a microwave just as when baking in a conventional oven.

SCONES Ⓕ

Cooking time: 3 minutes at FULL POWER

100 g/4 oz self-raising flour or plain flour with 1 level teaspoon baking powder
25 g/1 oz butter or margarine
25 g/1 oz light brown sugar
milk to bind

Sift the flour or flour and baking powder. Rub in the butter or margarine. Add the sugar and enough milk to make a soft rolling consistency. Roll out until about 1 cm/⅜ inch in thickness. Cut into 4 to 6 rounds. Arrange on a flat plate and cook for 3 minutes at FULL POWER until well risen. Allow to stand for several minutes. When the scones are cold, split and spread with butter.

For variety add 25 g/1 oz dried fruit or a little grated orange or lemon rind to flavour.

Variations

SAVOURY SCONES

Omit the sugar from the basic Scones recipe, and add a little seasoning to the flour.

CHEESE SCONES

Omit the sugar from the basic Scones recipe. Add seasoning and 25 to 40 g/1 to 1½ oz grated cheese to the mixture after rubbing in the butter or margarine.

COMPLETE MENUS

While you will undoubtedly use your microwave cooker in conjunction with a conventional oven and hotplates or boiling rings, there are many times when a complete meal can be prepared in a microwave cooker.

The fact that certain foods need to stand for several minutes after being cooked in the microwave means that an accompaniment or a second course can be placed into the microwave and cooked. Consider each menu and work out the best order of cooking. If you make full use of the microwave cooker, you will save an appreciable amount of fuel.

SPINACH AND BACON SALAD

TOMATO BAKED EGG

CARAMELLED ORANGE

Step 1.
Make the caramel sauce (see page 51) if this has not been prepared in bulk. Peel and slice a large orange, put into a dish, top with the warm sauce and allow to cool.

Step 2.
Chop a tomato, put into a ramekin dish and heat for a few seconds on FULL POWER. When the tomato is cold, break an egg on top, pierce the yolk, season lightly and add a spoonful of milk or cream. Cover the dish so that the egg does not dry. Put on one side ready to cook.

Step 3.
Cook the spinach for 1 to 2 minutes (see under Vegetables, page 44). Strain and chop. Prepare bacon while spinach is cooking.

Step 4.
De-rind and chop a bacon rasher. Cook on FULL POWER (see page 14), blend with the spinach and season well. Put onto a serving plate, cover and cook for 30 seconds on FULL POWER.

Step 5.
While you eat the Spinach and Bacon Salad, put the Tomato Baked Egg into the microwave cooker. This takes 2 minutes' cooking, so it is advisable to undercook slightly so that the egg completely sets during standing.

Step 6.
Serve the Caramelled Orange prepared earlier in Step 1.

JAMAICAN GRAPEFRUIT
CHILLI CON CARNE
RICE
GREEN SALAD
UPSIDE-DOWN PUDDING

Step 1.
Prepare the Chilli con Carne (see page 43). If this has been frozen, defrost in the microwave cooker. Do not overcook as it must be heated (see Step 7). Make the green salad.

Step 2.
Cook the rice (see page 11).

Step 3.
While the rice is cooking, make the mixture for the Upside-Down Pudding (see page 52). Put into the dish ready to cook.

Step 4.
Halve a grapefruit, loosen the segments of just one half and top with a little rum, a sprinkling of brown sugar and spice.

Step 5.
Remove rice from cooker. Allow to stand.

Step 6.
Heat the grapefruit for 30 seconds on FULL POWER and serve.

Step 7.
Heat the Chilli con Carne for 2 minutes on FULL POWER. Allow to stand until ready to serve with the rice and salad.

Step 8.
Put the pudding into the microwave while eating the main course.

FRENCH ONION SOUP
LIVER AND BACON
DUCHESS POTATOES
MIXED VEGETABLES
APPLE MERINGUE

Step 1.
Make the French Onion Soup (see page 21). Put on one side ready to reheat.

Step 2.
Prepare the vegetables and put ready to cook; make sure the cooking time is the same for all vegetables.

Step 3.
Bake a potato (see page 46). Halve, scoop out the potato pulp, blend with a little seasoning and 15 g/½ oz butter or margarine. Separate an egg, beat the yolk into the potato pulp, put the white into a basin for the meringue and spoon the Duchess Potato into a dish to reheat.

Step 4.
Bake the apple (see page 56) and remove the skin. Fill the centre with dried fruit if desired. Whisk the egg white, fold in the sugar and spoon over the apple. Set in the microwave (see method under Queen of Puddings page 55). Put on one side.

Step 5.
Heat the soup and serve.

Step 6.
Cook the vegetables prepared in Step 2, allow to stand (for details see page 44).

Step 7.
Cook the liver and bacon (see page 33). Allow to stand.

Step 8.
Heat the Duchess Potato for 1 minute. Serve the main course.

BEEF COBBLER
CAULIFLOWER
RASPBERRY TRIFLE

Step 1.
Make a custard sauce (see page 55). Split and fill a trifle sponge with raspberry jam; top with custard. When the custard is cool decorate with raspberries and whipped cream.

Step 2.
Prepare and cook the Bolognese Sauce or one of the other recipes based on Savoury Mince (see pages 42 and 43). Undercook by 2 minutes.

Step 3.
While the meat mixture is cooking, prepare the Savoury Scones (see page 57). Put two on one side to cook later. Place the other two uncooked scones on the hot meat mixture. Cook for 2 minutes on FULL POWER. Cover the dish and allow to stand.

Step 4.
Cook the cauliflower (see page 44).

POACHED FISH WITH PRAWN SAUCE
CREAMED POTATO
MIXED SALAD
FRESH FRUIT
WELSH RAREBIT

Step 1.
Defrost about 25 g/1 oz prawns if frozen; chop the prawns.

Step 2.
Make the salad, cover and keep in the refrigerator.

Step 3.
Cook a jacket potato, scoop out the pulp and mash with butter and milk (see page 46). Put into a small dish ready to reheat. Cover well.

Step 4.
Prepare the cheese for the Welsh Rarebit.

Step 5.
Make 150 ml/¼ pint White Sauce (see page 50), but use only 5 tablespoons milk, as the liquid used in poaching the fish will be added at stage 7.

Step 6.
Poach the fish (see page 26). Strain off the liquid, cover the dish containing the fish and allow to stand while completing the sauce.

Step 7.
Add the fish liquid to the sauce, with a little more milk if necessary, and the chopped prawns. Blend well. Heat on FULL POWER for 1 minute.

Step 8.
Pour the sauce over the fish and sprinkle with paprika.

Step 9.
Heat the creamed potato for about 30 seconds, or until very hot. Serve the fish with the potato and salad.

Step 10.
Make the Welsh Rarebit (see page 8).

MORE USES FOR YOUR MICROWAVE COOKER

This book has given a selection of recipes and hints for cooking various kinds of dishes. There are, however, a number of other ways in which your microwave cooker is invaluable.

Making preserves

You can prepare jams, jellies and chutney in a microwave cooker with great success. It is particularly suitable for cooking fairly small quantities of a particular preserve.

The technique of preparing a jam or jelly follows the conventional method. The fruit must be softened. The sugar must be stirred into the hot fruit or fruit juice in the case of a jelly, after which the jam or jelly must be allowed to boil rapidly until setting point is reached.

The proportions of fruit and sugar are the same as when making the preserve in an ordinary saucepan or preserving pan. When additional pectin, in the form of lemon juice, is required, use the same quantity as given in a standard recipe.

There is, however, one essential difference. Because the fruit softens more rapidly in a microwave cooker than in a preserving pan, you need half the quantity of water given in most standard recipes for jam or jelly.

The setting point for a jam or jelly is 104.5°C/220°F. This high temperature means that you must use a strong ovenproof or flameproof ceramic bowl that will withstand this heat and that it must be sufficiently large to allow the preserve to boil rapidly, without fear of its boiling over. Do not try to make too large an amount of jam or jelly at one time. Base this on 450 to 550 g/1 to 1¼ lb fruit.

The mixture of fruits and vegetables in chutneys can be softened easily and rapidly in a microwave cooker rather than in a saucepan. Due to the quicker cooking period, the ingredients retain the maximum flavour.

Making sweetmeats

Fudge and other sweetmeats can be cooked in a bowl in the microwave cooker instead of in an ordinary saucepan. Follow any standard recipe; there is no need to alter the proportion of the ingredients. The advice about the choice of bowl given under Preserves is even more important when making cooked sweetmeats for the temperature to which the mixture is cooked is extremely high.

Blanching vegetables

If you freeze vegetables, the initial blanching (short cooking period) is an important stage. Vegetables can be blanched in a microwave cooker in a shorter time than in a pan.

INDEX